My Light and My Salvation

365 daily devotional journal

BELLE CITY GIFTS

Belle City Gifts
Savage, Minnesota, USA
Belle City Gifts is an imprint of BroadStreet Publishing Group, LLC.
Broadstreetpublishing.com

My Light and My Salvation

9781424571253

Typesetting and design by Garborg Design Works | garborgdesign.com

Editorial services by Michelle Winger | literallyprecise.com

Printed in China.

25 26 27 28 29 30 31 7 6 5 4 3 2 1

Again the Lord of light and life
Awakes the kindling ray,
Unseals the eyelids of the morn,
And pours increasing day.
This day be grateful homage paid,
And loud hosannas sung;
Let gladness dwell in ev'ry heart,
And praise on ev'ry tongue.
Ten thousand different lips shall join
To hail this welcome morn;
Which scatters blessings from its wings
To nations yet unborn.

AGAIN THE LORD OF LIGHT AND LIFE
ANNA L. BARBAULD

Introduction

Are you longing to deepen your relationship with God and cultivate a more intentional devotional life? *My Light and My Salvation* is the perfect companion for your daily faith journey.

With carefully selected Scriptures, thought-provoking meditations, and guided prompts, this devotional journal will help you center your heart and mind on truth. Slow down, reflect, and align your thoughts with God's Word. As you do, take some time to journal your insights and prayers in the space provided.

Whether you're new to journaling or looking for a fresh approach to your daily devotions, this book will help you build consistent habits that keep you grounded in your spiritual walk. Make each day intentional. Lean into the wisdom and guidance of God and remember that he is your light and your salvation.

DAY 1

Something New

"I am about to do something new.
See, I have already begun! Do you not see it?"

ISAIAH 43:19 NLT

The first day of a new season is filled with an undeniable air of expectation. The excitement of a new outfit or gadget pales in comparison to the promise of a new beginning. Give God your plans. Keep him at the forefront of your mind as you make decisions.

How do you engage God in your plans?

DAY 2

All Things New

He who was seated on the throne said, "I am making everything new!"
Then he said, "Write this down, for these words are trustworthy and true."

REVELATION 21:5 NIV

As you begin a new day, empty and full of both promise and unknown, you can rest your soul in the truth that God will make everything new. Your regrets, mistakes, and failures are nothing compared to his covenanted promise of redemption and newness.

What new things do you want God to do with you?

DAY 3

Invisible

The LORD looks down from heaven and sees the whole human race.
From his throne he observes all who live on the earth.

PSALM 33:13-14 NLT

Have you ever felt invisible? Maybe you've felt like no one is on your side. The God of the entire universe sees you. He is always watching; he never sleeps or looks away. You have his attention. No matter how alone you feel, he is always aware of you.

How can you know that God sees you?

DAY 4

Patient Now

Be completely humble and gentle;
be patient, bearing with one another in love.

EPHESIANS 4:2 NIV

God's love for you isn't dependent on your success or how many mistakes you make. He loves you regardless of your status or class. Love others in the same way even when they mess up.

How can you show patience with others?

DAY 5

My Identity

Once you had no identity as a people; now you are God's people.
Once you received no mercy; now you have received God's mercy.

1 PETER 2:10 NLT

The world tells you to be true to yourself. In reality, you are called to be true to who God says you are. He is the one who defines you because he knows you best. Your identity is in Christ. You can walk confidently in his mercy and grace.

How can you know that God values you?

DAY 6

Not Your Own

I know, LORD, that our lives are not our own.
We are not able to plan our own course.

JEREMIAH 10:23 NLT

Put each of your days into God's hands. Let him direct you and guide you even when you go off course. It's never too late to listen to his gentle and wise voice. Talk to him about your plans, and wait for his response.

Do you trust God to direct and correct you? Explain.

DAY 7

Like Jesus

Our lives are a Christ-like fragrance
rising up to God.

2 CORINTHIANS 2:15 NLT

When you are following Jesus, God is pleased with you. He sees you the same way that he sees his Son. He is proud of you as you seek to follow Christ through all of your days.

How can you exhibit the character of God today?

REFLECTIONS OF THE WEEK

DAY 8

Untamable

Set a guard, O Lord, over my mouth;
keep watch over the door of my lips.

Psalm 141:3 NIV

Your mouth can get you into a lot of trouble. Ask God to help you be aware of the impact of your words. He will teach you how to speak wisely and kindly. Surrender to his guidance and let your words honor him.

How can you set a guard over your mouth?

DAY 9

Faith Matters

Because of Abraham's faith,
God counted him as righteous.

Romans 4:22 NLT

Even when the odds were stacked against him, Abraham believed that God was reliable. He trusted he would do what he said. God hears your prayers. Even if you cannot hear his response, you can believe that he is working!

How can you put your faith into action today?

DAY 10

The Fear Factor

When I am afraid, I will put my trust in you.
I trust in God, so why should I be afraid?

Psalm 56:3-4 NLT

Are you holding onto fear today? Are you magnifying a concern into an impossible mountain of what ifs? Trust Jesus. Remember his promises to you. No matter the outcome, he is on your side!

How can you give God your fear today?

DAY 11

Remember

I recall all you have done, O Lord;
I remember your wonderful deeds of long ago.

Psalm 77:11 NLT

Remembering what God has done builds your faith. Each time he proves himself faithful to you, another brick in the foundation of trust is laid. The precedent has been set that he is reliable, and he will do what he says. Don't forget all the ways he has worked in your life.

How has God been faithful to you?

DAY 12

Mercy over Sacrifice

"Go and learn what this means,
'I desire mercy and not sacrifice.'"

MATTHEW 9:13 CSB

It can be tempting to try and live a life worthy of God's approval. Success and failure alike can define who you think you are. This is not how you are supposed to live. God cares more about Christ's sacrifice for you than he does your own good works.

How can you rely on Christ's sacrifice today?

DAY 13

Give and Get

A generous person will prosper;
whoever refreshes others will be refreshed.

PROVERBS 11:25 NIV

Being generous can feel scary. Can you really give freely without worrying about your own needs? God's Word assures you that you can. When you refresh others, God promises that you will be refreshed. He sees each act of generosity.

How can you be generous today?

DAY 14

Necessary Faith

Without faith it is impossible to please God, since the one who draws near to him must believe that he exists and that he rewards those who seek him.

HEBREWS 11:6 CSB

Pleasing God requires that you trust what he says is true even if you don't understand. When you trust in what you cannot see, you demonstrate an ability to lean on God's understanding over your own.

Where is your faith level?

REFLECTIONS OF THE WEEK

DAY 15

Born of God

As many as received Him, to them He gave the right
to become children of God.

John 1:12 nkjv

Just like knowing who your earthly parents are gives you a sense of identity, so does knowing who your heavenly Father is. Realizing that you are a child of God can change everything you believe about yourself. As his child you are chosen, royal, fully loved, and fully known.

Do you see yourself as a child of God?

DAY 16

Go to God

Hear me when I call, O God of my righteousness!
You have relieved me in my distress.

Psalm 4:1 nkjv

When you are in distress, who do you call? Instead of running to a spouse, friend, or mentor, call upon the Lord. Cast your cares on him. It is good to be near the Lord when you need help.

Do you believe in God's ability to take care of you? Explain.

DAY 17

Rejoice Always

Rejoice always, pray continually, give thanks in all circumstances; for this is God's will for you in Christ Jesus.

1 THESSALONIANS 5:16-18 NIV

Life doesn't always work out the way you want it to. The circumstances that you find yourself in can leave you feeling disappointed and even resentful. Don't let the details of your life impact your habit of praising God. He is always worthy of your praise.

What can you praise God for today?

DAY 18

Courage for Christ

It is my eager expectation and hope… Christ will be honored in my body, whether by life or by death.

PHILIPPIANS 1:20 ESV

Paul knew that the Christ he preached was offensive to many people; the gospel was very hard for others to accept. But he was confident that the truth about Jesus was worth telling. He is a great example of counting the cost and striving to live a life that honors God.

How do you count the cost of being a Christ follower?

DAY 19

Undeserved Gift

The grace of God has appeared
that offers salvation to all people.

TITUS 2:11 NIV

You are saved by grace. Your salvation is not earned or accredited. You can live a life that honors what Christ has done for you by receiving his gift and striving to live out his example of holiness.

How do you say no to ungodliness?

DAY 20

Unshakable

Since we are receiving a kingdom that cannot be shaken, let us be thankful,
and so worship God acceptably with reverence and awe.

HEBREWS 12:28 NIV

When you think of the current political climate, do you think of words like *steady*, *strong*, and *reliable*? It's hard to imagine a kingdom as perfect and unshakable as God's. No matter what is happening in the world around you, you have good things to look forward to.

What does an unshakable kingdom look like to you?

DAY 21

Crown of Life

Blessed is the man who remains steadfast under trial,
for when he has stood the test he will receive the crown of life.

JAMES 1:12 ESV

God doesn't promise an easy life. He does, however, promise a great reward to those who endure. He promises the crown of life for those who don't give up. He is close to you no matter what your struggle is. Lean on him and he will give you the strength to carry on.

How can you stay focused on the crown of life?

REFLECTIONS OF THE WEEK

DAY 22

Name Above All

You have exalted your name and your promise
above everything else.

Psalm 138:2 CSB

It is good to remember that God's name is higher than any other. Ask the Holy Spirit to show you any area in your life that you have placed too much value on. He will guide you with kindness to a place of repentance.

How can you honor God with the way that you live?

DAY 23

Clothed in Grace

Put off your old self, which is being corrupted by its deceitful desires;
to be made new in the attitude of your minds.

Ephesians 4:22-23 NIV

Your life in Christ is meant to be free from the power of sin and death. If you feel like you have been caught wearing sin like an ugly old garment, take it off! Instead, clothe yourself with an attitude of forgiveness and the freedom that was given to you through Jesus.

How can you embrace the freedom Jesus purchased for you?

DAY 24

Call on Him

You, God, see the trouble of the afflicted;
you consider their grief and take it in hand.

PSALM 10:14 NIV

God is your great helper. He sees the lonely, the abused, the hungry, and the hurting. He carefully watches over his children and is close to those heavy with grief. He offers his hand to any who would call on him. You are never alone in your pain.

What do you need God for today?

DAY 25

No Longer Captive

You did not receive the spirit of bondage again to fear,
but you received the Spirit of adoption by whom we cry out, "Abba, Father."

ROMANS 8:15 NKJV

Jesus' death allows you to go from your former life of captivity to a life of freedom and light. When you truly understand your freedom, you can begin to let go of the areas of your life that hold you back.

Is part of your heart still stuck in fear?

DAY 26

Call Me

"Call to me and I will answer you,
and I will tell you great and mighty things, which you do not know."

JEREMIAH 33:3 NASB

God wants you to call on him, and he tells you that he will answer. You don't have to question his availability or wonder if he hears you. Confidently ask for help; he will be faithful to respond.

What do you need God to hear today?

DAY 27

Good Discipline

LORD, how happy is anyone you discipline
and teach from your law.

PSALM 94:12 CSB

Discipline is often followed by tears, so it might seem surprising when the Bible associates discipline with happiness! The truth is that you can rejoice in discipline because God is the perfect judge and teacher. He knows exactly what is best for you. His discipline is always good and right.

What discipline are you grateful for?

DAY 28

Without Complaint

Do everything without grumbling or arguing, so that you may become blameless and pure, children of God.

PHILIPPIANS 2:14 NIV

There will always be something to complain about. Without even trying, you can probably list a handful of things you're currently bothered by. The real effort comes in seeking to live with a heart of gratitude.

What can you stop complaining about today?

REFLECTIONS OF THE WEEK

DAY 29

At the Crossroads

"Stop at the crossroads and look around. Ask for the old, godly way, and walk in it. Travel its path, and you will find rest for your souls."

JEREMIAH 6:16 NLT

There will be times in life when your choices aren't obvious. When a crossroad appears, God is near. He wants to help you navigate your life. Ask him for wisdom and direction and follow his lead.

What choice do you need wisdom for today?

DAY 30

Beautiful Layers

Make every effort to add to your faith goodness; and to goodness, knowledge.

2 PETER 1:5 NIV

Your relationship with Jesus began with faith. As you walk with him, you will become more like him. He will teach you goodness, self-control, perseverance, and godliness. Let your faith grow into a life that honors the Lord.

What beautiful layers of faith can you see in your life?

DAY 31

Praise the Creator

It was you who set all the boundaries of the earth;
you made both summer and winter.

PSALM 74:17 NIV

In his great wisdom, God created the seasons. He knows when his creation needs the warmth of the sun and the solace of winter. He holds the earth in his hands and knows what's going on in each corner of your world. Rest in the infinite wisdom and ability of the Creator.

What creativity can you thank God for today?

DAY 32

Built Up

Encourage one another and build one another up,
just as you are doing.

1 THESSALONIANS 5:11 ESV

It is important for you to belong to a healthy community of believers. Your church needs you to encourage its members, and you need your fellow brothers and sisters in Christ to do the same for you.

How can you encourage someone in your church today?

DAY 33

Approved

Go, eat your bread with joy, and drink your wine with a merry heart,
for God has already approved what you do.

ECCLESIASTES 9:7 ESV

You don't have to wonder if God is pleased with you; your identity through his Son is enough to warrant his full blessing, his true approval, and his fierce love. Jesus' sacrifice is more than enough to cover your wrongdoings and mistakes.

Do you think God is pleased with you? Explain.

DAY 34

Been with Jesus

They were amazed. Then they realized that
Peter and John had been with Jesus.

ACTS 4:13 NCV

Peter and John acted like Jesus because they spent so much time with him. When you spend time with Jesus, it's inevitable that you'll become more like him. His presence is transformative.

What changes when you spend time with Jesus?

DAY 35

The Watching World

You lavish it on those who come to you for protection,
blessing them before the watching world.

Psalm 31:19 NLT

How often do you go to God for what you need? He gives you all of that, but he doesn't stop there. He also gives you his goodness, his kindness, his love. His provision for you goes far beyond your practical or physical needs.

What has God blessed you with lately?

REFLECTIONS OF THE WEEK

DAY 36

Choose Joy

Always be joyful. Pray continually, and give thanks whatever happens.
That is what God wants for you in Christ Jesus.

1 THESSALONIANS 5:16-18 NCV

You can choose to be joyful even when things aren't going the way you want. No matter your circumstances, you can lift them up to the Lord. He wants to walk with you and help you navigate whatever you're going through.

How can you choose joy today?

DAY 37

Illuminated

"Anyone who lives by the truth comes to the light,
so that his works may be shown to be accomplished by God."

JOHN 3:21 CSB

The Bible says that those who believe in Jesus are not condemned! His sacrifice means that you get to live in the light even though you did nothing to deserve it. The more time you spend with Jesus, the more you'll desire to live a life that honors him.

Are you living in the light?

DAY 38

Softly Spoken

A soft answer turns away wrath,
But a harsh word stirs up anger.

PROVERBS 15:1 NKJV

Are you guilty of reacting harshly when someone speaks angrily or unfairly to you? You probably know that your reaction didn't help the issue. Ask God to help you speak softly. He will give you the wisdom to know how to communicate best.

What does answering softly look like for you?

DAY 39

Faithful with Few

"You have been faithful with a few things;
I will put you in charge of many things."

MATTHEW 25:21 NIV

There may be parts of your life that don't look the way you want. Even in those areas, you can remain faithful to God. You can honor him in whatever is put before you. When you seek to do his will, there is no task that is too small. Nothing goes unnoticed.

How can you be faithful in the little things?

DAY 40

Ready to Help

The LORD God is my strength;
He will make me walk on my high hills.

HABAKKUK 3:19 NKJV

When you need strength, God is there to help. God can help you find your way through anything that life throws your way. He is always available and ready to guide you. All you have to do is ask.

Do you trust God to guide your steps?

DAY 41

Shepherd

"I am the good shepherd. The good shepherd
lays down his life for the sheep."

JOHN 10:11 CSB

Jesus said that he is the Good Shepherd, and it is good to remind yourself that you absolutely need him. Without Jesus you are lost. Without his sacrifice and guidance, you would have no way to be close to God.

How has the Good Shepherd guided you?

DAY 42

His Spirit in You

God has not given us a spirit of fear,
but of power and of love and of a sound mind.

2 TIMOTHY 1:7 NKJV

Without Christ, you are bound to a life of fear, weakness, hatred, and confusion. It is by his Spirit alone that you can love others, trust in his wisdom, and believe faithfully in the truth.

How do you rely on God's Spirit in your life?

REFLECTIONS OF THE WEEK

DAY 43

He Is Faithful

All of God's promises have been fulfilled in Christ
with a resounding "Yes!"

2 CORINTHIANS 1:20 NLT

God is a promise keeper. Everything he has spoken has come to pass. He is faithful to keep his Word. This means that if he says you are forgiven, you are. If he says he will be near to you, he will.

How have you seen the faithfulness of God in your life?

DAY 44

Bravery

"Be strong and courageous. Do not be afraid; do not be discouraged,
for the LORD your God will be with you wherever you go."

JOSHUA 1:9 NIV

When you become a follower of Jesus Christ, his bravery becomes your own. Through his grace and in his power, you are able to face the obstacles in your life with strength. Your mighty God goes before you and after you.

How courageous do you feel today?

DAY 45

Growing in Love

As we live in God,
our love grows more perfect.

1 JOHN 4:17 NLT

Love is hard. It means sacrificing your own priorities for those of another. It goes against your natural instinct. Without God, true love is impossible. You need his heart to effectively love others.

How can you grow in your love for others?

DAY 46

Not Disappointed

You will be rewarded for this;
your hope will not be disappointed.

PROVERBS 23:18 NLT

Are you familiar with the sting of disappointment? It hurts to hope for something and watch it wither away. Know that there is one hope that will never be lost. The hope that you place in Jesus is never misplaced. He will do exactly what he says.

What are you hoping for today?

DAY 47

I Am Yours

See what great love the Father has given us
that we should be called God's children—and we are!

1 JOHN 3:1 CSB

You are a child of God, and nothing can change that truth. Whether you feel worthy or not, you were created in his image, and you are fully loved. He is delighted that you are part of his family.

How does being adopted into God's family feel to you?

DAY 48

Kindness Always

Instead, be kind to each other, tenderhearted, forgiving one another,
just as God through Christ has forgiven you.

EPHESIANS 4:32 NLT

God's word is clear about how to treat others. You are called to be kind, patient, and forgiving. This can be hard to do! Ask God to help you see those around you the way that he does.

How can you be kind to someone today?

DAY 49

On Level Ground

Teach me to do your will, for you are my God;
may your good Spirit lead me on level ground.

Psalm 143:10 NIV

Just because you love God doesn't mean you will aways know what to do or how to live. This is why it's important to rely on the wisdom and guidance of the Holy Spirit. If you trust him, he will be faithful to teach you his will.

How are you learning God's will?

REFLECTIONS OF THE WEEK

DAY 50

Much Comfort

We share in the many sufferings of Christ. In the same way,
much comfort comes to us through Christ.

2 Corinthians 1:5 NCV

In this life, you might see or experience great suffering. Thankfully, God isn't lofty or distant. There is no better comforter than someone who has been exactly where you are. When you are heavy with sorrow, let the God of all comfort be near to you.

What do you need comfort for today?

DAY 51

Precious

"Because you are precious to me, because I give you honor and love you,
I will give other people in your place;I will give other nations to save your life."

Isaiah 43:4 NCV

Do you know how precious your life is to God? His love for you is unending. It is so great that he willingly gave up his only Son so that you could be close to him. He moved heaven and earth so that you would have a way to be near to him.

Is it hard for you to accept this truth?

DAY 52

Great Faith

Peter said, "Lord, if it is really you, then command me
to come to you on the water."

MATTHEW 14:28-29 NCV

Sometimes God might ask you to do something that doesn't make sense. Not every path he asks you to walk will be clearly defined or easy to navigate. But if you keep your eyes on him, you can walk across the most tempestuous waters as if they were simply solid ground.

How can you move toward Jesus in faith today?

DAY 53

He Hears

If we know that he hears us—whatever we ask—
we know that we have what we asked of him.

1 JOHN 5:15 NIV

God loves his children. He is a good Father who is always available. He is never bothered or inconvenienced by your needs. He wants to hear from you, and he loves it when you ask for help. In all circumstances, call on him. He is delighted by your voice.

What are you asking God to hear today?

DAY 54

Held Captive by Fear

When you lie down, you will not be afraid;
Yes, you will lie down and your sleep will be sweet.

PROVERBS 3:24 NKJV

Fear can overwhelm your mind, causing anxious thoughts and sleepless nights. Instead of giving in to your fears, trust that God can handle them. Cast your fears upon him and know that he is big enough to deal with them. Let him replace your fears with peace because you trust in him.

What fears are you handing to Jesus right now?

DAY 55

Truly Special

You are a chosen people, a royal priesthood,
a holy nation, God's special possession.

1 PETER 2:9 NIV

Long before you existed in your mother's womb, you were set aside and marked as special. You were chosen to be God's special possession, and that's pretty amazing. Embrace that truth and walk confidently into your day.

Whose opinion matters the most to you?

DAY 56

Ordered Steps

I will instruct you in the way you should go;
I will counsel you with my loving eye on you.

Psalm 32:8 NIV

Just as a toddler relies on the steady hand of a parent to walk across the room, so you can rely on the steady hand of God. He promises to show you which way to go. He will be faithful to guide you if you let him. Don't be stubborn and try to do it on your own.

How are your steps ordered?

REFLECTIONS OF THE WEEK

DAY 57

Temptation

Great is our Lord and abundant in strength;
His understanding is infinite.

Psalm 147:5 NASB

When you approach God to ask for help, you don't have to worry about how he will react. His understanding is infinite. He is full of wisdom, and he is a perfect judge. He doesn't see the way you do. His ways are so much higher. You can approach him with great confidence.

How do you think God reacts to your requests for help?

DAY 58

Limitless

Again and again they limited God, preventing him from blessing them.
Continually they turned back from him and wounded the Holy One!

Psalm 78:41 TPT

God has no capacity; he is without limits. He tells you that in him, anything is possible. You don't need to have confidence in what you can do—only in what he can accomplish through you. Don't be afraid to trust God for big, miraculous things in your life. He is more than able.

What big things are you asking God for?

DAY 59

Never Alone

"Surely I am with you always,
to the very end of the age."

MATTHEW 28:20 NIV

God is always with you. He promises that he is always near. You don't ever have to worry about being alone or abandoned because the one who made you is always close. He will never give up on you and never leave you to fend for yourself.

How does it feel to know God won't leave you alone?

DAY 60

Make Room

"He must become greater and greater,
and I must become less and less."

JOHN 3:30 NLT

When you accept Christ's sacrifice and the Holy Spirit takes up residence in your heart, you make room. Old habits must make way for fresh, new ways of being. As his presence grows inside you, the old ways diminish.

How do you make room for Jesus in your heart?

DAY 61

Time for Comfort

He comforts us in all our troubles
so that we can comfort others.

2 Corinthians 1:4 NLT

You have probably experienced seasons when you need God's comfort and peace more than the air you breathe. If that's you today, let his comfort wash over you. Let him be near to you in your suffering. One day, God will use your suffering to bring hope to others.

How have you been able to comfort others?

DAY 62

Waiting

The ransomed of the Lord will return and come to Zion with singing,
crowned with unending joy.

Isaiah 35:10 CSB

The sin and sadness of life can make waiting for Christ's return seem endless. Don't lose heart. He is coming for you! You are not forgotten; your pain is familiar to him. Keep your eyes fixed on him, and he will help you run your race with perseverance.

What have you been eagerly waiting for?

DAY 63

Overwhelming Devotion

This forever-song I sing of the
gentle love of God overwhelming me!

Psalm 89:1 TPT

God's faithfulness is firm. He is steady and can be counted on. You don't question whether or not the sun will rise. You depend on it and are convinced daily that it will happen. In the same way, lean on the Lord. Trust in him because he has proven himself trustworthy.

Do you fully trust God?

REFLECTIONS OF THE WEEK

REFLECTIONS

REFLECTIONS

DAY 64

Lifting the Veil

Whenever anyone turns to the Lord,
the veil is taken away.

2 CORINTHIANS 3:16 NIV

As you turn to the Lord, he will continuously reveal his truth. The more time you spend with God, the more you will understand his character and his heart. He brings clarity, understanding, and wisdom everywhere he goes.

What veil do you need lifted today?

DAY 65

Many Witnesses

Since we are surrounded by such a great cloud of witnesses, let us throw off everything that hinders and the sin that so easily entangles.

HEBREWS 12:1 NIV

When you are discouraged in your faith, take a look at those who have gone before you. Learn from the faith of other believers. Be encouraged by their successes and comforted by the evidence of God's mercy in their lives. Let that motivate you to godliness as well.

What witnesses are you particularly grateful for?

DAY 66

You Are Beautiful

You are altogether beautiful, my darling;
there is no flaw in you.

SONG OF SONGS 4:7 NIV

If God says that you are beautiful, then you can trust that is the truth. He does not lie, exaggerate, or embellish his words to make you feel good about yourself. You are created in his image, and he is pleased with you.

When do you feel most beautiful?

DAY 67

Sunshine and Storm

When times are good, be happy; but when times are bad, consider this:
God has made the one as well as the other.

ECCLESIASTES 7:14 NIV

True joy comes when you can see the value hidden in your darkest hours—when you can sing his praises no matter what. You don't know what the future holds for you here on earth, but you do know that your eternity is secure. He holds all of your days in his hands.

What value have you seen in your storms?

DAY 68

Lighthouses

"You are the light of the world.
A town built on a hill cannot be hidden."

MATTHEW 5:14 NIV

Jesus is the light of the world. That light is meant to be shared not hidden. You are called to shine brightly for him in such a way that others can see who he is. When you walk like he did, you can't help but share his light with those around you.

How can you share your light today?

DAY 69

Like You Mean It

"Everything is possible
for one who believes."

MARK 9:23 NIV

There's no need to pray weak, nervous, or timid prayers. God already knows what you need, and he is fully capable of providing for you. Go to him boldly, like a child who is confident in the goodness of their father. Remember that he loves to give good gifts to his children.

What can you ask boldly for today?

DAY 70

Pieced Together

He heals the wounds
of every shattered heart.

Psalm 147:3 TPT

No matter the hurts you carry, or the ones you are currently walking through, the Lord can heal you. He can take a shattered heart and piece it back together. After all, he is the one who made you. He knows exactly how to fix what is broken.

Where do you need to be pieced back together?

REFLECTIONS OF THE WEEK

DAY 71

Greatest Delight

Make God the utmost delight and pleasure of your life,
and he will provide for you what you desire the most.

Psalm 37:4 TPT

God is meant to be the greatest delight of your life. The world will throw many temptations your way, but your heart was made to be satisfied only by God. As alluring as money, fame, success, or relationships seem, you will never be satisfied until you are satisfied in the Lord.

Are you satisfied in the Lord?

DAY 72

In Every Step

The steps of the God-pursuing ones follow firmly in the footsteps of the Lord.
And God delights in every step they take to follow him.

Psalm 37:23 TPT

God delights in every step you take to follow him. It doesn't say that God delights only in your big leaps of faith or your consistent pace. No, he delights in every single small step that you take to follow him. He's delighted by every glance his way and every act of worship.

What steps are you taking to follow God?

DAY 73

Choosing Wisdom

If you wait at wisdom's doorway, longing to hear a word for every day,
joy will break forth within you as you listen for what I'll say.

PROVERBS 8:34 TPT

If you ask for wisdom, you will get it. God's Word promises that it is a gift he is always willing to give. In any situation, you have access to the best possible opinion. Don't try and manage on your own when you have such a great gift available to you at all times.

What does choosing wisdom look like for you today?

DAY 74

Notice the Weary

May the God who gives endurance and encouragement give you
the same attitude of mind toward each other that Christ Jesus had.

ROMANS 15:5 NIV

There is so much to be gained in relationship with other believers, whether on the receiving or giving end. Lift up those around you, notice when they are weary, and support them as you all seek to run your race well.

How can you encourage the weary today?

DAY 75

Soak in Truth

Truthful words stand the test of time,
but lies are soon exposed.

PROVERBS 12:19 NLT

There is an enemy who wants to steal, kill, and destroy. One of the most powerful ways he does that is by telling lies about who God is. If you fill your mind with the truth of Scripture, you won't be as prone to believe those lies.

How do you soak in the truth?

DAY 76

Confident

It is not that we think we are qualified to do anything on our own.
Our qualification comes from God.

2 CORINTHIANS 3:5 NLT

There is great freedom in admitting your shortcomings and allowing the Father to be your strength. You can be confident in your incompetence, and you can be equally confident in God's great strength and ability. He is more than qualified to carry out his plans.

How are you confident in God's strength?

DAY 77

Be Delighted

O my son, give me your heart.
May your eyes take delight in following my ways.

PROVERBS 23:26 NLT

God is consistently pursuing his children. He wants to be close to you. He wants a relationship with you. He made you, and he knows you full well. He knows what is best for you, and he wants to lead you through all of your days.

How do you delight in following God's ways?

REFLECTIONS OF THE WEEK

DAY 78

Conscious Choice

"Today I have given you the choice between life and death, between blessings and curses."

DEUTERONOMY 30:19 NLT

You have the conscious ability to choose whether or not you will love God. God will not make you love him or force you to follow him. He doesn't want anyone trapped, tricked, or forced to follow him. You get to decide.

What conscious choice are you making today?

DAY 79

Free from Offense

"I have swept away your offenses like a cloud, your sins like the morning mist. Return to me, for I have redeemed you."

ISAIAH 44:22 NIV

It can be hard to understand the grace offered by God because you are incapable of giving that kind of grace yourself. But when God says that he has forgotten your sin, and that he has made you new, he really means it. He sweeps your offenses away and never brings them up again.

Do you understand the grace of God?

DAY 80

Never Forsaken

"I will bring the blind by a way they did not know;
I will lead them in paths they have not known."

Isaiah 42:16 NKJV

God did not create you and then leave you alone. He does not expect you to figure out life all by yourself. He wants to lead you and help you navigate each and every one of your days. He does this because he loves you. He won't leave you alone because he loves to be with you.

How do you feel God leading you?

DAY 81

Breathe Easy

When hard pressed, I cried to the Lord;
he brought me into a spacious place.

Psalm 118:5 NIV

Life is full of pressures and stress. Each day you can find multiple reasons to be overwhelmed, annoyed, or discouraged. Take your pressures to the Lord. Cast them upon him and let him fill you with peace. Cry out to him and let him take your burdens from you.

What do you need to give to God so you can breathe easy?

DAY 82

Remain in Me

"The one who remains in me and I in him produces much fruit,
because you can do nothing without me."

JOHN 15:5 CSB

God says that the only thing you need to do to bear fruit is to remain in the vine. If you stay close to him, he promises to nurture you and sustain you. He also promises to prune you. The pruning isn't for the sake of staying small. It is so you can bear even more fruit.

What fruit are you bearing right now?

DAY 83

Work Well

Whatever you do, do well. For when you go to the grave,
there will be no work or planning or knowledge or wisdom.

ECCLESIASTES 9:10 NLT

Every day you wake up is a new opportunity to go about your day with excellence. Whether you are in meetings at work or dropping kids off at school, you can honor the Lord in the way that you live. No matter what your task, seek to do it well, glorifying God.

What can you work well at today?

DAY 84

He Hears

The eyes of the LORD are on the righteous,
and his ears are attentive to their cry.

PSALM 34:15 NIV

God's ears are attentive to you. He is aware of you, and he hears you when you call for him. He will not leave you alone when you ask for help. He is always willing to give his attention to his children. He is never annoyed, too busy, or bothered by your questions.

What do you want to tell God today?

REFLECTIONS OF THE WEEK

DAY 85

Call for Help

My help comes from the LORD,
who made heaven and earth.

PSALM 121:2 NCV

Life is full of trouble. It's inevitable that some of your days will be difficult. No matter what comes your way, you have the maker of heaven and earth on your side. He is always ready to help you. Call out to him and let him lead you through whatever you are facing.

What do you need help with today?

DAY 86

His Words

Your word is a lamp to guide my feet
and a light for my path.

PSALM 119:105 NLT

God's Word is an incredible gift. Don't let it be an untapped resource in your life. Fill your mind with it and let it soak deep into your heart. No matter the circumstance, God's Word will lead you the right way.

What are you currently reading about in God's Word?

DAY 87

He Is Risen

"You are looking for Jesus the Nazarene, who was crucified. He has risen! He is not here. See the place where they laid him."

MARK 16:6 NIV

Jesus has risen! You know that this is true. Your whole faith is based on it. Yet sometimes it's easy to forget the magnitude of it. Let the miracle of Christ's resurrection encourage you today.

What do you feel when you ponder the resurrection of Christ?

DAY 88

Young Spirit

That is why we never give up. Though our bodies are dying, our spirits are being renewed every day.

2 CORINTHIANS 4:16 NLT

No matter the state of your health, your spirit can stay young in Christ. No sickness or weariness can take away the life that you have in Jesus. No matter how your body feels, you can feel vibrant and alive when you are living by the Spirit.

How young does your spirit feel?

DAY 89

Love Endures

Love never gives up, never loses faith, is always hopeful,
and endures through every circumstance.

1 Corinthians 13:7 NLT

Be kind to the person you see in the mirror, to the one you might not think is worthy of love. God loves you, inadequacies and all. He sees you through the lens of a father who loves without conditions or expectations.

How does God's enduring love change your perspective?

DAY 90

Every Part

O my people, trust in him at all times.
Pour out your heart to him, for God is our refuge.

Psalm 62:8 NLT

God is waiting for you to pour out your heart to him. There isn't any part of you that scares him or that he is ashamed of. He already knows the deepest parts of you. Nothing can surprise him. Trust him with every part of you.

What can you trust God with today?

DAY 91

Morning Cry

In the morning, LORD, you hear my voice;
in the morning I lay my requests before you and wait expectantly.

PSALM 5:3 NIV

Each morning presents a new opportunity to meet with the Lord. You can begin your day by telling him what you need and trusting that he has it handled. It is not your job to fret or figure it out. Lay your requests before him and wait expectantly today.

What are you asking God for today?

REFLECTIONS OF THE WEEK

DAY 92

Sincere Heart

Let us draw near to God with a sincere heart and
with the full assurance that faith brings.

HEBREWS 10:22 NIV

Draw near to God with a sincere heart. Come to him honestly, just as you are. He doesn't need you to figure yourself out first. It's only in his presence that you'll find a clean conscience and the forgiveness of sins.

What is on your sincere heart today?

DAY 93

Sufficient Grace

It is only by God's grace
that you have been saved!

EPHESIANS 2:5 NLT

You cannot boast in your salvation. There is nothing you have done to deserve the eternal life that you have with Jesus. You know beyond a shadow of doubt that his grace is the only thing sufficient for you.

How do you thank God for his undeserved gift of grace?

DAY 94

Walking Honorably

The name of the Lord Jesus will be honored because of the way you live,
and you will be honored along with him.

2 THESSALONIANS 1:12 NLT

The secret to living a life that honors God is found in depending heavily on his grace to cover you. Do what you know is right. Don't compromise. Humbly ask God for help and he will show you the way to go when you are unsure.

How can you walk honorably today?

DAY 95

Hope in God

May the God of hope fill you with all joy and peace as you trust in him,
so that you may overflow with hope by the power of the Holy Spirit.

ROMANS 15:13 NIV

The Lord is gracious and kind. In his wisdom and justice, he would have every reason to require you to live a certain way and give nothing in return. Yet, he showers you with joy, peace, and hope. He gives good gifts freely to his children.

Are you filled with the hope of God?

DAY 96

Word Is Alive

The word of God
is alive and powerful.

HEBREWS 4:12 NLT

God gave his Word for your edification, education, and inspiration. Whatever you are going through, the Word of God holds the answers. Fill your heart with the truth found in Scripture and you will remain close to the Lord all of your days.

What part of God's Word comes alive to you today?

DAY 97

Find Happiness

Make me walk along the path of your commands,
for that is where my happiness is found.

PSALM 119:35 NLT

Seeking happiness is a sure way to get lost. You might think you can figure out exactly what you need and how it will make everything better, but the truth is that happiness lies in following the path that God has for you. His ways are the best ways.

How do you look for happiness?

DAY 98

The Judge

"The Rock, his work is perfect, for all his ways are justice.
A God of faithfulness and without iniquity, just and upright is he."

DEUTERONOMY 32:3-4 ESV

God is a perfect judge. He alone is qualified, and he alone is truly just. He doesn't see the way you do. Every situation, every conflict, every troubled heart is clear to him. His ways are perfect. When you face troubles, go to the perfect judge for guidance.

What do you need the perfect Judge to help you with today?

REFLECTIONS OF THE WEEK

DAY 99

Walk Away

"Those who were ready went in with him to the marriage feast, and the door was locked."

MATTHEW 25:10 NLT

Perseverance depends on your preparation. Have you stored up enough oil for the trials to come? Or will you have to walk away, unprepared, before the bridegroom's return? Continue putting your faith in the one who made you, and you will endure.

How can you fill your lamp today?

DAY 100

My First Love

"I have this against you, that you have abandoned the love you had at first."

REVELATION 2:4 ESV

All you need is the Lord. As you run your race, seeking to endure, don't forget that you once turned to the Lord in both desperation and admiration. Let your heart be soft and keep your eyes steadily on him. Remember the love you've felt for him in the past.

How can you make God your first love?

DAY 101

Keep Waiting

If we hope for what we do not see,
we eagerly wait for it with patience.

ROMANS 8:25 CSB

It's hard to wait for God's timing. Even when you are waiting for good things, you don't want to wait for long. God's Word says that waiting is a benefit. Hope is a blessing. Be patient and trust that God has the best timing.

What are you hoping for?

DAY 102

Free to Do

Do not use your freedom to indulge the flesh;
rather, serve one another humbly in love.

GALATIANS 5:13 NIV

Followers of Jesus are challenged to see freedom differently than the world. The world will tell you to pursue whatever makes you feel good. God's Word says to serve others in humility. Instead of indulging your every desire, think about what those around you need.

How can you use your freedom to serve others?

DAY 103

Mercy Covers

The LORD is good to all,
and his mercy is over all that he has made.

PSALM 145:9 ESV

Have you ever laid in bed thinking about past sin and beating yourself up over decisions you made years ago? You are not alone. Most people are incredibly hard on themselves. Remember that God's mercy covers all of your wrongs. His goodness is your salvation.

How can you trust in God's mercy today?

DAY 104

Fully Equipped

His divine power has granted to us everything
pertaining to life and godliness.

2 PETER 1:3 NASB

You are probably keenly aware of your weaknesses. Thankfully, you don't have to depend on your own strength. God is the one who gives you what you need to live. He equips you to live a godly life and fills you with the knowledge of who he is.

How are you equipped to live a godly life?

DAY 105

Grace upon Grace

Of His fullness we have all received,
and grace upon grace.

John 1:16 NASB

Even when your circumstances are ordinary or difficult, God's love is full, and his grace is boundless. The goodness that he wants to pour on you has no end. Each day you follow him you have access to the undeserved grace you desperately need.

What do you need grace for today?

REFLECTIONS OF THE WEEK

DAY 106

Spirit Is Willing

I know that nothing good dwells in me, that is, in my flesh;
for the willing is present in me, but the doing of the good is not.

Romans 7:18 nasb

You might know the right thing to do but struggle with the execution. It's not always easy to do what is right. You're not alone in this struggle. Don't be discouraged; instead, remember that God has fully equipped you to live a godly life.

What right thing are you trying to do right now?

DAY 107

Humble Favored

He gives us more grace. That is why Scripture says:
"God opposes the proud but shows favor to the humble."

James 4:6 niv

God gives grace to the humble because the humble are keenly aware of their need for him. When you walk in humility, you gladly admit that without him you can do nothing. Don't be fooled into thinking you are strong enough on your own.

How can you walk in humility today?

DAY 108

Everything Possible

It is God who makes us able to do
all that we do.

2 CORINTHIANS 12:9 ESV

When it comes to living a life that honors the Lord, you don't have to be willing and able. You can just be willing because God is able. God continuously does miraculous things through the weakness of his children.

What impossible tasks can you give to God today?

DAY 109

Glorify Him

His divine power has given us everything we need for a godly life through our knowledge of him who called us by his own glory and goodness.

2 PETER 1:3-4 NIV

By God's power, you have everything you need for a godly life. He has not left you empty handed. He has called you to glorify him and has fully provided you with the means to do it.

How can you bring glory to God today?

DAY 110

Approach with Confidence

Let us come boldly to the throne of our gracious God. There we will receive his mercy, and we will find grace to help us when we need it most.

HEBREWS 4:16 NLT

There is usually protocol to seeing royalty. Not everyone is given the ability to walk into a throne room. This isn't true with God. Despite being the one true King, he invites you to approach him unhindered.

Are you boldly approaching the King today?

DAY 111

Steady and Strong

The LORD is compassionate and gracious,
Slow to anger and abounding in lovingkindness.

PSALM 103:8 NASB

It is good to be near to the Lord. He is slow to anger and overflowing with kindness. He is a safe refuge for you when your emotions are like a raging storm. No matter how you feel, he is consistent, steady, and gentle.

Do you need a safe refuge for your emotions today?

DAY 112

Not Fearful

Such love has no fear,
because perfect love expels all fear.

1 JOHN 4:18 NLT

At the end of the age, on judgment day, you don't need to be afraid. You don't need to worry what God will say or be nervous that you won't pass the test. Be confident in Christ's work on the cross that covers you fully.

How does God's love alleviate your fear?

REFLECTIONS OF THE WEEK

DAY 113

Take Refuge

Be my rock of refuge, to which I can always go;
for you are my rock and my fortress.

PSALM 71:3 NIV

God is the rock on which you can firmly plant your hopes. When you rely on him, you will not be shaken. You will be steady and strong because he is steady and strong, reliable in the fiercest storm. There is nothing stopping you from taking refuge in his arms when you need it.

What hopes are you planting on the rock?

DAY 114

Faith in Storms

He said to his disciples, "Why are you so afraid?
Do you still have no faith?"

MARK 4:39-40 NIV

Even though they witnessed Christ's power day after day, the disciples still doubted him. They saw him with their own eyes and still struggled to understand. Imagine the compassion that the Lord has for you as you seek to walk in faith. You trust in what you cannot see.

What storms do you need faith for right now?

DAY 115

Finding Contentment

I have learned in whatever situation
I am to be content.

PHILIPPIANS 4:11 ESV

The key to unlocking contentment amidst the trials is in trusting that your needs have been met and will continue to be met. Contentment grows, no matter your circumstances, when you have the right perspective on where your blessings come from.

Are you content in your current situation? Explain.

DAY 116

The Right Path

Make me to know your ways, O LORD;
teach me your paths.

PSALM 25:4 ESV

Trusting God for guidance is not normal. The world will tell you to take your own path, do what you want, seek what feels good. Instead, humbly ask God what he wants from you. Trust in him to show you the way to go.

Are you on the right path?

DAY 117

Being Courageous

May he give you the power to accomplish all the good things our faith prompts you to do.

2 THESSALONIANS 1:11 NLT

When you place your trust and hope in God, he will give you the courage you need to do the tasks he wants you to do. Maybe you need courage to have a difficult conversation or to walk through your day without giving in to anxiety. No matter what's before you, God will equip you.

What do you need courage for today?

DAY 118

Depending On God

Be strong and courageous. Do not be afraid or terrified… for the LORD your God goes with you; he will never leave you nor forsake you.

DEUTERONOMY 31:6 NIV

Through every unpredictable situation, through all disappointments, delays, and disruptions, you can cling confidently to the faithfulness of God. He is the one solid rock on which you can firmly stand. No matter what uncertainty you are facing, God is with you.

How do you show your dependence on God?

DAY 119

Stay the Course

Everyone who competes in the games goes into strict training. They do it to get a crown that will not last, but we do it to get a crown that will last forever.

1 CORINTHIANS 9:25 NIV

There comes a time in every race when your ability hits a wall, and you simply need the resolve to not quit. Living a life that honors the Lord is like that as well. You must go beyond what you are capable of, beyond what makes sense. If you don't quit, you win.

How can you determine to stay the course?

REFLECTIONS OF THE WEEK

DAY 120

Truth Over Feelings

"When you pass through the waters, I will be with you,
and the rivers will not overwhelm you."

ISAIAH 43:2 CSB

Do not doubt the truth; God cares for you deeply. No matter how you might feel, God is with you. He promises that he will guide you through every trouble that you face. You can trust that he will keep that promise.

How can you trust the truth over your feelings today?

DAY 121

Big Picture Confidence

"As the heavens are higher than the earth, so are my ways higher
than your ways and my thoughts than your thoughts."

ISAIAH 55:9 ESV

God has access to the big picture of your life. Trust that he sees exactly how each day is interwoven with the next. You don't have to make sense of every little thing. Rely on his ways, and he will see you through.

What excites you about God's ways?

DAY 122

Protected

You, O Lord, are a shield about me,
My glory, and the One who lifts my head.

Psalm 3:3 NASB

God is your shield and your strength. He is the one who protects you and keeps you safe. His presence is the safest place that you can be. When calamity comes, stay near to him. No matter what trouble you face, he is capable of handling it.

How protected do you feel today?

DAY 123

A Lofty Goal

I eagerly expect and hope that I will in no way be ashamed,
but will have sufficient courage.

Philippians 1:20 NIV

Declare the truth of this Scripture over your life today. What a lofty and noble goal to glorify God no matter what happens to you or around you. If this is your aim, God will equip you to fulfill it. Keep your eyes on him and he will see you through.

What lofty goals are you pursuing?

DAY 124

He Responds

I waited patiently for the LORD;
he turned to me and heard my cry.

PSALM 40:1 NIV

When you are desperate, God hears your cry. When you feel forgotten, he comforts you. And when you are wicked and depraved, he cleanses you of your offenses and makes you suitable for glory. No matter your state, God is attentive to you.

What are you asking God to respond to today?

DAY 125

All Things Beautiful

He has made everything beautiful
in its time.

ECCLESIASTES 3:11 NIV

God's Word says that he makes all things beautiful in his time. All things. Whatever situation you are facing right now, it has the potential to create beauty in you. Perseverance, humility, grace, obedience—these are beautiful things that can come from overcoming adversity.

What beauty do you see in your life?

DAY 126

Remember the Foundation

Through Christ you have come to trust in God.
And you have placed your faith and hope in God.

1 PETER 1:21 NLT

Don't forget the foundations of your faith! You are able to be near to God because of what Jesus did on the cross. Through his sacrifice you are righteous and able to dwell with God for all of eternity.

When was the last time you thanked Jesus for his sacrifice?

REFLECTIONS OF THE WEEK

REFLECTIONS

REFLECTIONS

DAY 127

Unmatched Faithfulness

Your lovingkindness, O Lord, extends to the heavens,
Your faithfulness reaches to the skies.

Psalm 36:5 NASB

Even when you are unfaithful, God is not. He is steady and dependable all of the time. It can be hard to grasp this kind of consistency, but it is true. God's faithfulness has no end. Don't measure God's faithfulness by your lack!

How has God been faithful to you recently?

DAY 128

No Quarrels

What is causing the quarrels and fights among you?
Don't they come from the evil desires at war within you?

James 4:1 NLT

God is consistent in the way that he says to treat others. He wants you to highly esteem those around you, use your words to speak life, and faithfully encourage them to love God with all that they have.

How can you love others today?

DAY 129

Free Creation

Creation itself will be set free from its bondage to corruption and obtain the freedom of the glory of the children of God.

Romans 8:21 esv

When Jesus returns all of creation will be set free. Imagine the kind of glorious perfection you will see in the world around you. No more tears, no more war, no more draught, and no more death. Everything will be in alignment with God's original design.

What do you most look forward to in the new creation?

DAY 130

Never Hidden

"Here I am! I stand at the door and knock. If anyone hears my voice and opens the door, I will come in and eat with that person."

Revelation 3:20 niv

God is not far away. He is not hiding from you, and he is not difficult to find. He promises that if you look, you'll see him. If you ask, he will answer. He has always kept his promises and he always will.

Are you looking for God today?

DAY 131

Just Ask

"If you believe, you will receive
whatever you ask for in prayer."

MATTHEW 21:22 CSB

If you are unaware of your need, you won't ask for help. It's such a simple equation that is often overlooked. You will only depend on God if you realize how desperately you need him. God always helps those who ask.

What will you ask God for today?

DAY 132

My Guide

All the paths of the Lord are steadfast love and faithfulness,
for those who keep his covenant and his testimonies.

PSALM 25:10 ESV

Life doesn't always feel smooth. Unexpected obstacles, daily stress, and even trauma can make you feel like you just can't catch a break. The truth is no matter how many bunny trails or dead ends you navigate, if you are trusting in God, he will keep you steady.

How do you stay steady?

DAY 133

Healer

"Daughter, your faith has made you well;
go in peace and be healed of your affliction."

Mark 5:34 NASB

The woman in the crowd had suffered for more than a decade. It's likely she had already tried everything she knew of to fix her issues. She was well aware that man's solutions weren't sufficient. She needed something more, something supernatural. She believed Jesus would heal her, and he did.

What healing are you believing for?

REFLECTIONS OF THE WEEK

DAY 134

My Hope

There is surely a future hope for you,
and your hope will not be cut off.

Proverbs 23:18 NIV

When doubt, discouragement, or despair threatens your soul, take heart. No matter what your days on earth look like, God has secured a future for you. As his child, you inherit his kingdom. You will dwell with him in eternity forever.

What hope are you clinging to?

DAY 135

Radiant Commands

The precepts of the Lord are right, giving joy to the heart.
The commands of the Lord are radiant, giving light to the eyes.

Psalm 19:8 NIV

God's intentions for the way you should live and his commands are wonderful. They aren't meant to be an impossible list or a burden too heavy to carry. When you follow Jesus closely, and live in a way that honors the Lord, you will have a heart full of joy and light in your eyes.

Do you find God's commands radiant? Explain.

DAY 136

By Name

Lord, you know everything there is to know about me.
You've examined my innermost being with your loving gaze.

Psalm 139:1 TPT

God knows your deepest need, your most painful wound, and your darkest thoughts. He is familiar with every single part of you, and he loves you all the same. There is nothing about you that could ever surprise him or catch him off guard.

How does being known by God make you feel?

DAY 137

My Joy

Be truly glad.
There is wonderful joy ahead.

1 Peter 1:6 NLT

God never promised that life would be easy. What he does promises that he will be with you at all times and that the best is yet to come. There is wonderful joy ahead. You can walk through trials knowing that one day, everything will be made right.

What brings you joy?

DAY 138

Always Fair

He did not retaliate when he was insulted, nor threaten revenge when he suffered. He left his case in the hands of God, who always judges fairly.

1 Peter 2:23 NLT

Life isn't fair. People will let you down, disappoint you, and even betray you. Instead of carrying the burden of justice, cast your cares upon the Lord. In your darkest moments, let him carry your burdens. He is far more capable of handling the situation than you are.

What do you need God to carry for you today?

DAY 139

His Hand

Though they stumble, they will never fall,
for the Lord holds them by the hand.

Psalm 37:24 NLT

When you need it, God's hand is available. He is there to steady you when you waver, comfort you when you are discouraged, and guide you when you are lost. God delights in extending his hand to you. Reach out today and know that he is there.

What does taking God's hand look like for you today?

DAY 140

He Is Love

We love because
he first loved us.

1 JOHN 4:19 ESV

Loving others is only possible when you love like God loves. If you love out of your humanity, sin gets in the way. Obeying the command to love begins with God's love. When you realize how great his love is, you can extend that undeserved love to others.

How do you show God's love to others?

REFLECTIONS OF THE WEEK

DAY 141

His Ways

His delight is in the LORD's instruction,
and he meditates on it day and night.

PSALM 1:2 CSB

The world will tell you that following your heart will make you happy. They'll tell you that the most important thing is doing what makes you feel good. The truth is that real, lasting happiness comes from following the ways of God. His instructions are good.

How do you delight in God's instruction?

DAY 142

The Teacher

"The Advocate, the Holy Spirit, whom the Father will send in my name,
will teach you all things and will remind you of everything I have said to you."

JOHN 14:26 NIV

The Holy Spirit is God's great gift. Jesus knew that his disciples would struggle after he left, so he gave them a Teacher. You can also rely on the Holy Spirit. He will remind you of truth and teach you how to live.

What is the Holy Spirit teaching you?

DAY 143

Persevere

Let us run with perseverance the race marked out for us,
fixing our eyes on Jesus.

Hebrews 12:1-2 NIV

Following Jesus isn't easy, and there will be times you will be tempted to quit. Another believer might hurt you, you might get tired of the narrow path, or you might be tempted to live in a way that you know isn't honoring to God. Don't quit! A great reward is coming.

How can you persevere today?

DAY 144

My Prayers

I call on you God, because you will answer me;
listen closely to me; hear what I say.

Psalm 17:6 CSB

Have you ever asked a question you already know the answer to? It changes the way you ask. The same is true with God. You can pray boldly and confidently because you know without a doubt that he is listening.

What are you praying for today?

DAY 145

Unblemished

Because of our faith, Christ has brought us into this place
of undeserved privilege where we now stand.

ROMANS 5:2 NLT

You were created to be in close relationship with God. Christ's death on the cross removed all that hinders you. He provided you with the ability to confidently stand before the Lord, unblemished and unashamed.

How does it feel to know you are unblemished?

DAY 146

His Job

Teach me your ways, O LORD,
that I may live according to your truth!

PSALM 86:11 NLT

It's not your job to clean up your own mess. Christ's sacrifice is what paves the way for you to be near to God. The Holy Spirit's faithful work in your life is what transforms your actions and behaviors. The glory goes to God. Lean on him, not your own ability.

Are you trying to do God's job?

DAY 147

Your Purpose

The purpose in a man's heart is like deep water,
but a man of understanding will draw it out.

PROVERBS 20:5 ESV

You are meant to play a beautiful and important role in God's eternal kingdom. You've been blessed with the skills and passion to fulfill God's purposes both here on earth and in his kingdom forever. Ask God for understanding, and he will show you your purpose.

What do you think your purpose is?

REFLECTIONS OF THE WEEK

DAY 148

Repent and Return

Repent and return, so that your sins may be wiped away, in order that times of refreshing may come from the presence of the Lord.

ACTS 3:19 NASB

Sin is exhausting. You cannot live an abundant life in Christ while still pursuing a life of sin. The beauty of salvation and the grace of God is that all you have to do is return to him in repentance and your sin will be erased.

Have you repented and returned to the Lord?

DAY 149

Gracious Words

Gracious words are like a honeycomb,
sweetness to the soul and health to the body.

PROVERBS 16:24 ESV

Your words are powerful. What you say can build others up or tear them down. Even the words you speak behind someone's back can have a tremendous effect on them. Commit to being the kind of woman who is overflowing with gracious words.

How can you speak with grace today?

DAY 150

Righteousness Poured Out

It is time to seek the LORD,
until he comes and showers his righteousness on you.

HOSEA 10:12 NIV

A day will come when you see your Savior face-to-face. You will dwell in the light of his presence for eternity. But for right now, you are in a season of seeking and preparing your heart for his coming glory. Ask him to keep your heart soft, so you can honor him with humility.

How can you keep your heart soft?

DAY 151

Reliable Promises

"Blessed is she who has believed that the Lord
would fulfill his promises to her!"

LUKE 1:45 NIV

You can trust wholeheartedly that God will do what he says. He says that he will redeem all that has been lost. He says that Jesus is coming back to make all things right. He says that the faith of his children will be rewarded. Don't lose sight of what he has promised you.

What reliable promises are you holding onto?

DAY 152

Something New

"In the same way I will not cause pain without allowing something new to be born," says the LORD.

ISAIAH 66:9 NCV

God always has a purpose. He doesn't ask you to weather a season of loss without preparing a place of peaceful restoration on the other side. If you are enduring a season of struggle, hold on to the promise that something new is being born out of your trial.

What new thing do you see on the horizon?

DAY 153

Miracle Worker

"Stop wailing," Jesus said.
"She is not dead but asleep."

LUKE 8:52 NIV

Imagine watching your child pass away only to have Jesus claim that she is asleep. There will be times in life when you are absolutely convinced of something, but God will tell you to believe differently. And he will always be right.

How can you trust God today?

DAY 154

Always Near

He did this so that they might seek God, and perhaps they might reach out and find him, though he is not far from each one of us.

ACTS 17:27 CSB

God wants to be with you. He promises that if you ask, you will receive, and if you look, you will find. He is near to those who search for him. If you are doubting his presence in your life because you cannot see him, ask God to strengthen your faith.

How close do you feel to God right now?

REFLECTIONS OF THE WEEK

DAY 155

True Children

We're no longer living like slaves under the law,
but we enjoy being God's very own sons and daughters!

GALATIANS 4:7 TPT

The King of all kings calls you his child. He wants to share everything he has with you. You are an heir to his kingdom, with full access to everything your Father has. All of his power, resources, and goodness are available to you.

How do you feel knowing you are an heir of God?

DAY 156

He Heals

I call to you from the ends of the earth
when my heart is without strength.

PSALM 61:2 CSB

No matter what wounds you are living with, the Lord is near. He is a loving, worthy, compassionate Father. He can bring healing to areas of your heart that have long been neglected. You are safe when you are in his care.

Do you feel God's nearness today?

DAY 157

His Attention

Let me see your face, let me hear your voice,
for your voice is sweet, and your face is lovely.

SONG OF SOLOMON 2:14 ESV

When you are overwhelmed, do you run to what makes you feel comfortable? It takes practice to learn to run to God first. He is the only one who can truly support you and give you what you need. Turn to him; his attention is already on you.

Do you feel God's attention on you?

DAY 158

Peaceful Sleep

In peace I will lie down and sleep, for you alone, LORD,
make me dwell in safety.

PSALM 4:8 NIV

When insecurity looms, the best place you can go is to God. When the darkness of night threatens to overwhelm you with fear or loneliness, know that God is with you. He will give you rest when you ask.

Is your sleep peaceful? Explain.

DAY 159

Constant Communion

Do not be anxious about anything, but in every situation,
by prayer and petition, with thanksgiving, present your requests to God.

PHILIPPIANS 4:6 NIV

No matter what your day brings, give it to the Lord. Bring him your needs, through prayer and petition, with thanksgiving. Ask him for what you need and thank him for all he is doing. Keep an open dialogue going with your Creator all throughout the day.

How do stay in communion with God?

DAY 160

Trust and Praise

"The LORD is my strength and my song, and he has become my salvation;
this is my God, and I will praise him."

EXODUS 15:2 ESV

Are you facing an impossible trial? Are you wondering where your strength to endure will come from? Does it seem absolutely crazy that God can and will lift you up to overcome? Remember that he is your strength and your song.

What are you trusting God for today?

DAY 161

The Right Foundation

Let your roots grow down into him, and let your lives be built on him.
Then your faith will grow strong in the truth you were taught.

COLOSSIANS 2:7 NLT

God is the rock on which you can confidently build. Storms will come, but he will see you through every trial and struggle. He will never leave your side and your faith will be strengthened.

Who is your foundation?

REFLECTIONS OF THE WEEK

DAY 162

True Support

My flesh and my heart may fail, but God is the strength of my heart and my portion forever.

PSALM 73:26 NIV

Life can be unpredictable. People fail, sickness overwhelms, and financial struggles suffocate. It can be tempting to think that everything would be better if only that one thing weren't an issue. God is your best and most reliable support. Nothing else will sustain you like he does.

How do you use God as your support?

DAY 163

All in All

I pray that from his glorious, unlimited resources he will empower you with inner strength through his Spirit.

EPHESIANS 3:14 NLT

God wants to strengthen you. He has exactly what you need today, and he does not hold back good gifts from his children. He is not sitting back, waiting for you to figure it out on your own. He wants to give you everything you need.

What do you need today?

DAY 164

Great Comforter

Blessed be the God and Father of our Lord Jesus Christ, the Father of mercies and God of all comfort, who comforts us in all our tribulation.

2 CORINTHIANS 1:3 NKJV

There are many ways that God comforts. His words can remind you of truth. His people can encourage you when you are down. He can meet you through a song or through nature. All of these are gifts straight from his heart.

How has God comforted you lately?

DAY 165

Love Well

"Administer true justice; show mercy and compassion to one another."

ZECHARIAH 7:9 NIV

The Scripture is full of reminders to show mercy and compassion to those in need. God has not forgotten them. He wants you to be kind and generous just as he is. Ask him to open your eyes to those around you who are hurting.

Who can you love well today?

DAY 166

Convinced of Love

I am persuaded that neither death nor life… nor any other created thing will be able to separate us from the love of God.

ROMANS 8:38-39 CSB

Nothing can separate you from the love of God. Jesus broke down all of the barriers when he died on the cross. There is not a single obstacle between you and the love of God. Nothing is in your way. Run to the Lord and embrace all that he has for you!

How convinced are you of God's love?

DAY 167

Discerning

This is my prayer: that your love may abound more and more in knowledge and depth of insight, so that you may be able to discern what is best.

PHILIPPIANS 1:9-10 NIV

God's Word promises that as you seek to love more, you will also grow in discernment. This means that you will know what to do and when to do it. If you're struggling to make decisions, ask God to help you grow in love and wisdom.

What do you need discernment for now?

DAY 168

More than Enough

God is able to make every grace overflow to you, so that in every way, always having everything you need, you may excel in every good work.

2 CORINTHIANS 9:8 CSB

You might feel like you don't have a lot to give. You may be stretched financially, emotionally, and mentally. This is not how God intended for you to live. He does not want you to be constantly stressed. Remember that he is able to provide abundance in your life.

How has God proven to be more than enough for you?

REFLECTIONS OF THE WEEK

DAY 169

Good Student

Every morning he wakes me.
He teaches me to listen like a student.

Isaiah 50:4 NCV

Every day is a new opportunity to learn from your Creator. You can walk in humility by reminding yourself that you will be a student forever. You don't have to worry about having it all figured out. Instead, lean on his wisdom and understanding.

What are you learning about God?

DAY 170

Complete Confidence

I rejoice, because I have
complete confidence in you.

2 Corinthians 7:16 ESV

Life and all of its messy circumstances can knock you off your feet and disintegrate even the most perfectly laid plans. Do not place your confidence in your own ability to maintain control. Instead, trust the Lord and rejoice that he is the one in charge.

Where does your confidence lie?

DAY 171

Establish Your Heart

You also be patient. Establish your hearts,
for the coming of the Lord is at hand.

JAMES 5:8 NKJV

Keep your eyes fixed on the return of Jesus. He is coming back to make all things right. As you anticipate that glorious day, fill your mind with truth. Keep your heart soft so you won't be offended on that day.

What do you most look forward to in the return of Jesus?

DAY 172

Purchased Freedom

He is so rich in kindness and grace that he purchased our freedom
with the blood of his Son and forgave our sins.

EPHESIANS 1:7 NLT

Your freedom came at a steep price. It's easy to recite the truth of the gospel, but how often do you actually let it sink in? God gave up his one and only Son for you. He died so you would be free!

Have you pondered the price of your freedom lately?

DAY 173

Always Speaking

"Son of man, let all my words sink deep into your own heart first.
Listen to them carefully for yourself."

EZEKIEL 3:10 NLT

God is always speaking to his children. If you're struggling to hear his voice, read the Word, look for his character in the world he created, or talk about his goodness with another believer. These are all ways you can learn to recognize who God is and what he is doing.

How has God been speaking to you lately?

DAY 174

He Will Succeed

I will exalt you and praise your name, for in perfect faithfulness
you have done wonderful things. things planned long ago.

ISAIAH 25:1 NIV

You can face trials with confidence when you remember that God has a victorious and assuredly successful plan. He has kept all of his promises and will faithfully redeem all that is broken.

How has God succeeded in your life?

DAY 175

Eternal Mercy

He has not punished us as our sins should be punished;
he has not repaid us for the evil we have done.

PSALM 103:10 NCV

The gospel isn't fair; you come out on top! There is nothing you could have done to earn your salvation. Without Christ's sacrifice, you would have been eternally lost. Praise the Lord for his eternal mercy and never-ending kindness.

How does God's eternal mercy affect each day?

REFLECTIONS OF THE WEEK

DAY 176

Believe This

"Everyone who lives and believes in me shall never die.
Do you believe this?"

JOHN 11:26 ESV

Do you really, truly believe that you will live forever in heaven with Christ? You are probably accustomed to promises being made and broken. Human fallacy may have left you skeptical. The beautiful truth is that you serve a God who will never back out of his covenant with you.

What do you believe?

DAY 177

Due Glory

LORD, you will grant us peace;
all we have accomplished is really from you.

ISAIAH 26:12 NLT

Have you climbed mountains and overcome trials? As you reflect on what you've been through, both good and difficult, do you give God the glory he is due? He is the one who carries your burdens, comforts your heart, strengthens your resolve, and orders your steps.

What glory can you give to God today?

DAY 178

Joy of Heaven

We do not focus on what is seen, but on what is unseen.
For what is seen is temporary, but what is unseen is eternal.

2 Corinthians 4:18 csb

It's not easy to fix your eyes on something you can't see. God can help you abandon your earthly perspective. Instead of being wrapped up in the anxieties of the world, you'll find yourself settled in the peace of knowing that this life is fleeting, and better things are coming.

Is the joy of heaven in your view?

DAY 179

Source of Joy

He will once again fill your mouth with laughter
and your lips with shouts of joy.

Job 8:21 nlt

God created laughter, and he is the source of true joy. Don't watch joy diminish as you get older! Let the God of all delight fill you with true joy. Give him your heavy heart and laugh without fear.

How much joy is in your life?

DAY 180

Father of Lights

He made the great lights;
his faithful love endures forever.

Psalm 136:7 csb

When you feel far from God, look for a sign that he is real and close. You will find proof. He made the sun, moon, and stars. The list is endless. Every single good thing in your life points back to the existence of a glorious Creator.

What proof do you have of God's goodness?

DAY 181

Lifted Leaders

Obey those who rule over you, and be submissive,
for they watch out for your souls, as those who must give account.

Hebrews 13:17 nkjv

God is fully aware of who your leaders are. He isn't surprised or dismayed by the people in power. You can rest knowing that God is your true authority. You can honor him by honoring your leaders.

What leader can you show honor to today?

DAY 182

Remedy

He gives strength to the weary
and increases the power of the weak.

Isaiah 40:29 NIV

What is the remedy for your weariness and weakness? Jesus. He is the one who can mend a broken relationship, lift up a discouraged spirit, and provide for all your needs. No matter what situation is causing you to feel weak, he is the one who will strengthen you.

What do you need Jesus to remedy for you?

REFLECTIONS OF THE WEEK

DAY 183

Unity

They all met together and were constantly
united in prayer.

ACTS 1:14 NLT

The early church is a great example of how to operate in unity. If you are part of a community of believers, then your presence and affirmation is needed. Don't let the enemy tell you that you are insignificant, or that you don't have a role.

What is your role in your community?

DAY 184

His Plans

Many are the plans in a person's heart,
but it is the LORD's purpose that prevails.

PROVERBS 19:21 NIV

When the world tells you to listen to your heart, remember that you are called to listen humbly to the Lord. His ways are higher. As his follower, don't seek what makes you feel good; instead, walk with the Lord and submit your desire to him.

What is the Lord saying to you?

DAY 185

Liberty unto Holiness

Now you are free from the power of sin.... Now you do those things that lead to holiness and result in eternal life.

ROMANS 6:22 NLT

You are free from the power of sin and death. You are no longer responsible for carrying the weight of your faults. Don't take that freedom and use it to do whatever you want. Instead, let your freedom push you to live a life that honors God and leads to holiness.

Are you living for holiness?

DAY 186

Lasting Love

Give thanks to the LORD, for he is good;
his love endures forever.

1 CHRONICLES 16:34 NIV

God's love never ends. You know this in your mind, but do you know it in your heart? It's hard to understand the concept of forever love. Be reminded today that God's love is secure and steady, incapable of changing or running out.

What does lasting love look like to you?

DAY 187

Human Likeness

Rather, he made himself nothing by taking the very nature of a servant, being made in human likeness.

PHILIPPIANS 2:7 NIV

Jesus knows what it is like to be human. He was hungry, tired, overwhelmed, and joyful. He was sad, excited, full of grief, and disappointed. He is no stranger to suffering. No matter what you are feeling, Jesus understands. He can comfort you because he has been there.

How do you picture Jesus as a human?

DAY 188

Praise in Crisis

About midnight Paul and Silas were praying and singing hymns to God, and the prisoners were listening to them.

ACTS 16:25 CSB

Being thrown into prison for your faith is one of the hardest forms of persecution believers can face. It is worth noticing that despite the walls around them, Paul and Silas continued to praise God with praying and singing. Even when the situation was dire, their faith was strong.

How do you praise in crisis?

DAY 189

Released and Restored

The punishment that brought us peace was on him,
and by his wounds we are healed.

Isaiah 53:5 NIV

Jesus suffered to release you from guilt. His punishment brought you peace. He wore your shame so you could be healed. While it is sobering to realize what Jesus has done, you can also rejoice in your freedom. Jesus is not still on the cross! Death did not win.

How do you rejoice in your freedom?

REFLECTIONS OF THE WEEK

REFLECTIONS

REFLECTIONS

DAY 190

Measured Days

"Lord, make me aware of my end and the number of my days
so that I will know how short-lived I am."

Psalm 39:4 CSB

Everyone has a limited number of days. No one knows how long they will live. By being mindful of your fleeting existence on earth, you can focus on the things that will last forever. Keep your eyes on what is eternal, and life's struggles won't carry as much weight.

How do you measure your days?

DAY 191

Not Shaken

Cast your burden upon the Lord and He will sustain you;
He will never allow the righteous to be shaken.

Psalm 55:22 NASB

When you bring your worry to God and lay your anxious heart bare before him, he will encourage you, lift you up, and sustain you. He will not allow you to be shaken or weakened by worry because he is capable of holding you securely through every situation.

What worry can you leave with Jesus today?

DAY 192

Never Disappointed

This hope will never disappoint us, because God has
poured out his love to fill our hearts.

Romans 5:5 NCV

No one is a stranger to being let down. But when it comes to your salvation, there is no need to brace for disappointment. The hope you have in Christ is guaranteed. He will never let you down.

What is the state of your hope?

DAY 193

Guided

"I will lead the blind by a way they did not know;
I will guide them on paths they have not known."

Isaiah 42:16 CSB

When you feel you have lost your way, God promises that he will lead you forward. Even if you can't see what lies ahead, God will guide you. It's not your job to navigate. Lean on the Lord, and he will see you through.

What is God guiding you into today?

DAY 194

God of Safety

"You are my place of safety and protection.
You are my God and I trust you."

Psalm 91:2 NCV

Whatever you are facing right now, God is more than able to rescue you and keep you safe. Remember his great power. Think of all the times, both biblically and in your own life, that God has faithfully protected his children. He will not let you down now.

How safe do you feel with God as your protector?

DAY 195

Cleansed

Wash me thoroughly from my iniquity,
And cleanse me from my sin.

Psalm 51:2 NKJV

In your cleansing, you are brought nearer to God. When you compare your sin to the treasure of closeness with the Father, it instantly loses its worth. Are there things in your life that you are holding onto instead of surrendering to God?

What do you want to be cleansed of today?

DAY 196

Without Fear

She is clothed with strength and dignity,
and she laughs without fear of the future.

PROVERBS 31:25 NLT

It's natural to fear the unknown. It can be frightening not to know what's coming or how to prepare for it. But you don't have to be afraid of the future when you know who you trust. You can live without anxiety about what is to come because you know that your life is in the hands of the one who controls it all.

What can you laugh about today?

REFLECTIONS OF THE WEEK

DAY 197

Greater Wonder

I look at your heavens, the work of your fingers,
the moon and the stars, which you have set in place.

Psalm 8:3 ESV

When you look into the night sky, you realize almost instantly how small you are in God's universe. The God who spoke the world into being is the same God who speaks quietly to your heart. His love is as unsearchable as the heavens.

When did you last ponder the greatness of God?

DAY 198

Trustworthy

The word of the Lord holds true,
and we can trust everything he does.

Psalm 33:4 NLT

God will never lie to you, manipulate you, or let you down. He will never go back on his word, abandon you, or stop loving you. Who he has been throughout the ages is who he is today.

How has God been faithful to you?

DAY 199

Secure in Truth

Those who love your teachings will find true peace,
and nothing will defeat them.

Psalm 119:165 NCV

When you are familiar with the truth, a lie doesn't have any power. You won't be discouraged by the lies of the enemy when you are sure of what's true. Understanding truth brings peace and contentedness.

How secure are you in the truth?

DAY 200

Joyfully Wait

I wait for the Lord, my whole being waits,
and in his word I put my hope.

Psalm 130:5 NIV

Waiting can be hard. But sometimes, waiting is wonderful. You can wait to deliver great news, wait for the birth of a child, or wait to give a special gift. This is how it is to wait for the Lord. Wait on him in joyful anticipation.

How can you joyfully wait for God?

DAY 201

Good and Perfect

Whatever is good and perfect is a gift coming down to us from God our Father, who created all the lights in the heavens.

JAMES 1:17 NLT

Pause and consider all the good, all the beauty, in your life. You may be in a season that makes this easy, or perhaps now is a time that doesn't feel particularly good or perfect. Flowers blooming, the wink of a quarter moon, loving and being loved, these are all gifts from God.

What gifts do you see today?

DAY 202

Tears to Joy

Those who sow in tears
shall reap with shouts of joy!

PSALM 126:5 ESV

Sometimes there are no words that bring comfort. No matter how well-intentioned the words, nothing takes away the ache. These are the times you need to crawl into your Father's lap and allow his love and promises to envelop you. He will restore your joy in time.

Can you rest in the Father's arms today?

DAY 203

Unconditional Acceptance

Accept one another, then, just as Christ accepted you,
in order to bring praise to God.

ROMANS 15:7 NIV

It's easy to list the ways other people could change for the better. It's easy to assume that the faults of others are what makes unity difficult. Instead of focusing on the weaknesses of those around you, ask God to soften your heart toward them.

How can you accept those around you?

REFLECTIONS OF THE WEEK

DAY 204

What Is Pleasing

God is working in you, giving you the desire
and the power to do what pleases him.

PHILIPPIANS 2:13 NLT

You can't conjure up the desire to honor God on your own. It is his work in you that gives you the desire to do what honors him. As you spend time with him and fill your mind with truth, you will know how to live like he wants you to.

How do you aim to please God?

DAY 205

Never Sleeps

He will not let you stumble;
the one who watches over you will not slumber.

PSALM 121:3 NLT

The one who watches over you never sleeps. He never takes a break. He doesn't shut his eyes even for a second. He does not miss a single thing. God makes sure you won't stumble as you climb today's mountain; he never stops watching.

How comforting is it to know that God never sleeps?

DAY 206

No Darkness

This is the message we have heard from him and declare to you: God is light; in him there is no darkness at all.

1 John 1:5 NIV

In total darkness, people instinctively seek light. They turn on their phones, fumble for a light switch, or light a candle. With a single light source, the darkness can be overcome. This same principle applies to your heart. God is pure light, and with him, you can overcome darkness.

How can you rely on the perfect light source today?

DAY 207

He Meets Needs

The Lord is all I need. He takes care of me.
My share in life has been pleasant; my part has been beautiful.

Psalm 16:5-6 NCV

God has exactly what you need. Maybe you're facing a situation that seems impossible. Take courage and be strong; nothing is impossible for him. Even when you can't see clearly, God always knows what is necessary, and he is able to help.

Which need of yours can God meet today?

DAY 208

You Are Chosen

God decided in advance to adopt us into his own family....
This is what he wanted to do, and it gave him great pleasure.

EPHESIANS 1:5 NLT

You are a part of God's family. No matter the state of your earthly family, you can find belonging with the Lord. He chose you and it delights him to be near to you. You are wanted and loved.

How do you feel about being chosen by God?

DAY 209

Sheltered

He will cover you with his feathers. He will shelter you with his wings.
His faithful promises are your armor and protection.

PSALM 91:4 NLT

Rest in this promise of protection. There is no need to wait, full of anxiety, for the next sign of trouble. Even when the night is dark, or a storm is raging, you are safe and secure. Take a deep breath and let God's promise of protection wash over you.

What are you seeking shelter from today?

DAY 210

Righteousness

The work of righteousness will be peace, and the effect of righteousness, quietness and assurance forever.

Isaiah 32:17 NKJV

To be righteous is to be in right standing before the Lord. This is why it says that Jesus is your righteousness. You can stand confidently before the Lord because of Christ's sacrifice. When you trust in Jesus, you will find peace, quietness, and assurance. Forever.

What does a righteous life look like to you?

REFLECTIONS OF THE WEEK

DAY 211

Wonder

As you do not know the path of the wind, or how the body is formed in a mother's womb, so you cannot understand the work of God.

ECCLESIASTES 11:5 NIV

You have access to whatever information you need most of the time. With this, you may have lost some of the ability to wonder. You don't have to have all the answers. You don't have to understand everything. That is God's job. Trust in his understanding instead of your own.

What causes you to wonder?

DAY 212

A Good Start

I rise before dawn and cry for help;
I wait for Your words.

PSALM 119:147 NASB

Numerous times in Scripture, you are encouraged to seek God in the morning. No matter what your day looks like, this is a good habit to form. It doesn't matter if you have an hour or a few minutes. Begin your day by acknowledging your Creator and asking for his guidance.

What is a good start to your day?

DAY 213

In Awe

No ear has perceived, no eye has seen any God besides you,
who acts on behalf of those who wait for him.

Isaiah 64:4 NIV

God is everlasting. He is the one true King. He has always been faithful, and he will continue to be. For time eternal, he is sovereign and glorious. There is no one like him, and there never will be.

What are you in awe of?

DAY 214

Seek Him

Devote your heart and soul
to seeking the Lord your God.

1 Chronicles 22:19 NIV

Maybe you are unsure of what your purpose is and how you should fulfill it. In times of doubt, you can always fall back on the truth that seeking God is your highest calling. No matter how the details play out, if this is your goal you'll always be on the right path.

What is your heart devoted to today?

DAY 215

Tell Your Story

Let the redeemed of the LORD tell their story—
those he redeemed from the hand of the foe.

PSALM 107:2 NIV

The story of your life is important. When you look back and see how each detail is interwoven, your faith is strengthened. Notice all the ways that God has been faithful to you. Remember his goodness and the way that he has carried you.

What story can you tell?

DAY 216

God of Restoration

The LORD raises up those who are bowed down;
The LORD loves the righteous.

PSALM 146:8 NASB

You serve a God of restoration. He is an expert at fixing what is broken, healing the sick, and giving life to the dead. He doesn't leave you to figure out your mess. He delights in being close. He loves to work in your life and show you his glory.

How is God restoring things in your life?

DAY 217

His Riches

This same God who takes care of me will supply all your needs from his glorious riches, which have been given to us in Christ Jesus.

PHILIPPIANS 4:19 NLT

God is capable of providing for all your needs. He is not limited, and he is not selfish. He knows precisely what is best for you. Through Jesus, you have access to all that God has to offer.

What riches has God shared with you lately?

REFLECTIONS OF THE WEEK

DAY 218

Better than Life

Because your love is better than life,
my lips will glorify you.

PSALM 63:3 NIV

Is God's love really better than life? If you're unsure, ask! Ask God to give you insight and understanding. Ask him to open your eyes to the things you don't relate to in his Word. He will be faithful to show you.

What do you need help understanding in God's Word?

DAY 219

Remember It All

My whole being, praise the LORD
and do not forget all his kindnesses.

PSALM 103:2 NCV

Do not forget the kindness of the Lord. Remember all that he has done for you. Bring to mind his faithfulness and dwell on how he saved you from the power of death. Ask God to remind you of all the ways he has shown up in your life.

What do you remember that God has done for you?

DAY 220

Any Prayer Counts

Pray in the Spirit on all occasions
with all kinds of prayers and requests.

EPHESIANS 6:18 NIV

There isn't a list of requirements you need to meet to talk to God in the right way. You don't have to have the right words, the right tone, or even the right attitude. Go to God; he can handle whatever you bring to him.

What are you coming to God with today?

DAY 221

Opportunity for Joy

When troubles of any kind come your way,
consider it an opportunity for great joy.

JAMES 1:2 NLT

Endurance is a quality that is crucial to staying true to your faith in the hard times. Rather than giving up when troubles come, hold onto your faith in Jesus and ask the Holy Spirit to help you in times of trouble.

What troubles can you use as an opportunity for joy?

DAY 222

Quenched

The desert and the parched land will be glad;
the wilderness will rejoice and blossom.

ISAIAH 35:1 NIV

Do you feel like you are always striving and never getting anywhere, thirsting for something more but still feeling dry? God is the one who can make a dry wilderness full of life. Go to him for the refreshing you need.

How can God quench your thirst today?

DAY 223

Always Light

Even in darkness light dawns for the upright,
for those who are gracious and compassionate and righteous.

PSALM 112:4 NIV

Life isn't always full of hope and joy, especially when you have experienced hurt, anxiety, or depression. Even in your darkest moments, God's light can shine. When you turn to him, he will keep you safe until morning.

How do you experience light in the darkness?

DAY 224

Thundering Voice

"God's voice thunders in marvelous ways;
he does great things beyond our understanding."

Job 37:5 NIV

With his voice, God created the heavens and the earth. With his voice, he faithfully led his people. With his voice, he calmed storms. That same voice speaks to you. He is powerful, strong, gentle, and kind all at once. Pay attention, and you will hear what he is saying.

How do you hear God's voice?

REFLECTIONS OF THE WEEK

DAY 225

Fiery Furnace

"If we are thrown into the blazing furnace, the God whom we serve is able to save us. He will rescue us from your power, Your Majesty."

DANIEL 3:17 NLT

You are unlikely to have to go through literal flames for God, but you have daily opportunities for your faith to impact the decisions you make. What you believe overflows from your heart and affects how you live.

How does your faith impact your decisions?

DAY 226

My Redeemer Lives

"I know that my Redeemer lives,
and at the last he will stand upon the earth."

JOB 19:25 ESV

God allowed Job to suffer in big ways. He lost his family, his health, and his wealth. Despite his great pain, Job held on to the truth that one day all would be perfect. He knew that what he lost wasn't lost forever. His faith was not in what he could see.

What is your faith placed in?

DAY 227

Contentment Always

I have learned the secret of being content
in any and every situation.

PHILIPPIANS 4:12 NIV

True contentment isn't found in obtaining the next thing you think you need. You don't need more to make you happy. The world will tell you that you don't have enough. Instead of listening, ask God to show you all the blessings you already have.

What are you content with today?

DAY 228

Search Me

Search me, O God, and know my heart;
Try me and know my anxious thoughts.

PSALM 139:23 NASB

You might be good at hiding things or convincing yourself that everything is fine. God sees clearly; he is not swayed by emotion or circumstance. He sees you exactly as you are and knows what is best for you. Trust him with your heart. He will hold it gently.

Do you trust God enough to share openly with him?

DAY 229

Steady Love

I love those who love me,
and those who seek me find me.

PROVERBS 8:17 NIV

With God, there is no such thing as unrequited love. God loves you far more consistently and fully than you could ever love him. His love for you is unending, and it cannot change. He will never lose interest or decide to move on. Turn to him and he will be faithful to you.

Have you experienced the steady love of God? Explain.

DAY 230

Continual Praise

From the rising of the sun to its going down
The LORD's name is to be praised.

PSALM 113:3 NKJV

Intentional, continual praise can only result in lasting joy. When you choose to look at each moment as a time in which to be thankful, you will also find beauty, joy, and satisfaction. Praise the Lord throughout your day and watch your perspective change.

How can you stay in an attitude of continual praise?

DAY 231

Gracious

The LORD longs to be gracious to you
therefore he will rise up to show you compassion.

ISAIAH 30:18 NIV

God doesn't long to show his anger or dole out punishments. He is not waiting for you to mess up so he can judge you without mercy and point out your flaws. He longs to be gracious to you. He is kind and waiting to show you compassion.

How has God been gracious to you?

REFLECTIONS OF THE WEEK

DAY 232

Better Things

"You also have sorrow now. But I will see you again. Your hearts will rejoice, and no one will take away your joy from you."

JOHN 16:22 CSB

One day Jesus will come back and make all things right. He will wipe away your tears and you will live in perfection for eternity. Put your hope in that day. When the pain of this life is too much, remember that it is not forever. Better things are coming.

What better things are you looking forward to?

DAY 233

Forgiven

"Do not turn aside from following the LORD, but serve the LORD with all your heart."

1 SAMUEL 12:20 ESV

Do you feel like you need to forgive yourself for your sin? Don't wallow in guilt and regret; forgiveness is not your job. Your sins have been taken care of. Rely on what Jesus says and continue serving him.

How do you know you have been forgiven?

DAY 234

Wholly Devoted

He alone is your God, the only one
who is worthy of your praise.

DEUTERONOMY 10:21 NLT

You were made to worship. If you don't worship God, you will find something else to take his place. Money, recognition, and success can easily become the highest priority. God alone is worthy of your praise. Does he occupy his rightful place in your life?

How do you show your devotion to God?

DAY 235

He Will Deliver

I wait for your deliverance, O Lord,
for your words thrill me like nothing else!

PSALM 119:174 TPT

It is good and right to wait on the Lord. He has promised to redeem you, and he is trustworthy. He will keep all of his promises. If there is brokenness in your life, surrender it to the Lord and trust his timing.

What hurts are you needing to be delivered from?

DAY 236

Enduring Hardship

Let perseverance finish its work so that you may be mature and complete, not lacking anything.

JAMES 1:4 NIV

The trials and hardships in life can seem unfair. Life should be comfortable and carefree, shouldn't it? Remember that your story is written by a compassionate Creator who is crafting a masterpiece. You can't always see his purpose, but you can trust that he knows best.

What are you enduring right now?

DAY 237

Eternity

We are citizens of heaven, where the Lord Jesus Christ lives. And we are eagerly waiting for him to return as our Savior.

PHILIPPIANS 3:20 NLT

God didn't design a broken world. It is natural to want something more. This world won't satisfy your soul. You were designed to live in perfection with Jesus. Let that longing in your heart propel you to live in a way that honors the Lord.

What do you long for?

DAY 238

Worth It

"I will make them walk by brooks of water, in a straight path in which they shall not stumble."

JEREMIAH 31:9 ESV

God sees you as you face each day. He knows why you cry, and he knows there is a deep longing in your heart for more. All of your longings will be fulfilled in eternity. You will be fully satisfied in his kingdom. Don't lose heart; the glory that is to come is worth every step.

Do you believe everything will be worth it in the end? Why or why not?

REFLECTIONS OF THE WEEK

DAY 239

Give Thanks

Enter his gates with thanksgiving and his courts with praise.
Give thanks to him and bless his name.

Psalm 100:4 CSB

As you praise God, your focus shifts from yourself to him. The gravity of whatever you are facing diminishes, even if just a bit, as you focus on something greater. Choose to worship him despite your circumstances because he is worthy.

How can you choose to worship God today?

DAY 240

The Helper

In the same way the Spirit also helps our weakness;
for we do not know how to pray as we should.

Romans 8:26 NASB

You might not always know what to pray. This is okay! Whether you are overwhelmed with emotion, lost in frustration, or just tired, you have an advocate who can help. The Holy Spirit can intercede for you. You don't have to have the perfect words to say.

What is on your heart today?

DAY 241

Protection of God

You have been a defense for the helpless, a defense for the needy in his distress,
a refuge from the storm, a shade from the heat.

Isaiah 25:4 nasb

In Christ, you are protected. You have a strong shield, a faithful defender, and a constant guardian. Storms will still rage, and suffering will still occur, but you can find solace knowing that God is on your side.

What storm do you need protection from today?

DAY 242

Specific Purpose

We are God's handiwork, created in Christ Jesus to do good works,
which God prepared in advance for us to do.

Ephesians 2:10 niv

You were formed by God. He created you, and he knows you better than anyone else. He knows exactly how you operate. If you are struggling to know your purpose, ask your Creator. He will show you what you were made for.

What were you made for?

DAY 243

Stay Faithful

Let us not grow weary of doing good, for in due season we will reap,
if we do not give up.

Galatians 6:9 esv

If you don't quit, you win. A lot of this journey to follow Jesus is about learning perseverance. Hold on to the end, don't lose faith, keep your eyes fixed on the Lord. When your faith is tested, let God strengthen you and guide you instead of giving up.

What are you enduring right now?

DAY 244

He Will Answer

When he calls out to me, I will answer him;
I will be with him in trouble.

Psalm 91:15 csb

When you call to God, he will answer you. He won't leave you alone in your trouble. He doesn't expect you to figure things out on your own. He wants to meet you, rescue you, and give you everlasting life.

When did you last call out to God?

DAY 245

Strength Every Morning

LORD, be gracious to us; we long for you.
Be our strength every morning, our salvation in time of distress.

ISAIAH 33:2 NIV

Each morning is an opportunity for you to commit your day to the Lord. He is your strength and your salvation. Start your day by being near to him and asking for his perspective. He will guide you and lead you faithfully.

Have you asked God for strength today?

REFLECTIONS OF THE WEEK

DAY 246

Burden Bearer

"I took the load off their shoulders;
I let them put down their baskets."

PSALM 81:6 NCV

God is a willing and able burden bearer. He is fully equipped to handle whatever is weighing you down. Your responsibility is to let him do it. Cast your concerns, worries, fears, and doubts into God's mighty hands and let him do the heavy lifting.

Can you let God bear your burden today?

DAY 247

Always Shining

"You are the light of the world.
A city set on a hill cannot be hidden."

MATTHEW 5:14 ESV

Though Satan will try, the light of Christ cannot be hidden. It cannot be contained, covered up, or snuffed out. It will continue to shine brightly in a dark world until the day that Jesus comes back and makes all things right. When you are discouraged, look for his light.

How is God's light shining through you today?

DAY 248

Bad News

They will have no fear of bad news;
their hearts are steadfast, trusting in the Lord.

Psalm 112:7 NIV

Living in the information age means bad news is prevalent. You can see what's happening around the world at any given time. It's easy to become discouraged and overwhelmed. Instead, trust in the Lord. Remember that his plans will succeed. Trust that he is in control.

How steadfast is your heart?

DAY 249

Read and Do

"They are those who, hearing the word, hold it fast in an honest and good heart,
and bear fruit with patience."

Luke 8:15 ESV

Don't just read the Word of God. Hear it and do what it says. God promises that when you follow his commands with an honest heart, you will bear fruit. If you just read it, nothing changes. Growth requires action.

What have you read in God's Word lately?

DAY 250

Eyes Open

Stay alert! Watch out for your great enemy, the devil.
He prowls around like a roaring lion, looking for someone to devour.

1 Peter 5:8 NLT

There is no reason to be afraid of the tactics of the enemy. If you pay attention, you will see them clearly. When you ask, the Holy Spirit will give you the discernment you need to walk wisely and to stand firm. Keep your eyes open and don't lose heart.

How are your eyes open to the schemes of the enemy?

DAY 251

Strong Faith

Faith is the confidence that what we hope for will actually happen;
it gives us assurance about things we cannot see.

Hebrews 11:1 NLT

Faith is what keeps you going when trials happen. When everything around you seems grim and the future is uncertain, faith will carry you through. This is why God rewards faith. He knows that sometimes you want to quit. Hold fast. Let your faith be strengthened.

How strong is your faith?

DAY 252

His Opinion

You, Lord, are our Father.
We are the clay, you are the potter; we are all the work of your hand.

Isaiah 64:8 NIV

God is your Creator. He knows you perfectly—every strength and every flaw. If you struggle with insecurity, ask God to open your eyes to the way he sees you. He will be faithful to show you.

Whose opinion matters most to you?

REFLECTIONS OF THE WEEK

REFLECTIONS

REFLECTIONS

DAY 253

Held Together

He is before all things,
and in him all things hold together.

COLOSSIANS 1:17 NIV

Do you struggle with wanting to be in control of various aspects of your life? It is not your job to hold everything together. Your responsibility is to submit to God and trust that he is fully capable of weaving the details of your life together. Lean on the one who is really in control.

Do you struggle to let God be in control of your life?

DAY 254

Joy

Do not grieve, for the joy of the LORD
is your strength.

NEHEMIAH 8:10 NIV

In the book of Nehemiah, the people grieved when they heard the Word of God read aloud after more than seventy years. There was conviction, sorrow, and an understanding of their sin. Instead of grieving, Nehemiah said to be joyful, to celebrate their atonement and be glad.

How can you be joyful in repentance today?

DAY 255

Fear

Fear of man will prove to be a snare,
but whoever trusts in the LORD is kept safe.

PROVERBS 29:25 NIV

Fear is a liar that holds you back from experiencing all God has for you. You cannot lean on the Lord fully and walk in fear at the same time. Fear tells you to protect yourself and take matters into your own hands. Trust puts control back into the hands of God where it rightly belongs.

How can you choose not to live in fear today??

DAY 256

Follow the Light

"I am the light of the world. Whoever follows me will never walk in darkness,
but will have the light of life."

JOHN 8:12 NIV

If you follow Jesus all of your days, you will never walk in darkness. When you stay close to him, you will see clearly and be confident in the path before you. You won't stumble around or get lost. You will walk securely in the light.

How are you following the light in your life?

DAY 257

Enduring Mercy

Oh, give thanks to the LORD, for He is good!
For His mercy endures forever.

PSALM 106:1 NKJV

God's mercy endures forever. You can't quantify it, and you won't ever be able to test its limits. There is no end to the mercy of God. He will consistently, forever, love you in a way that you don't deserve.

How does God's enduring mercy affect you today?

DAY 258

Waiting

Wait for the LORD;
Be strong, and let your heart take courage.

PSALM 27:14 NASB

It's not always easy to wait but when it comes to the Lord, it is worth it. If you are waiting for something and are becoming impatient, resentful, or weary, ask God to give you a glimpse of his heavenly perspective. He will strengthen your faith and help you when you ask.

What are you eagerly waiting for?

DAY 259

Songs of Victory

You are my hiding place; you protect me from trouble.
You surround me with songs of victory.

PSALM 32:7 NLT

God is your hiding place—your protection and your rest. He walks with you through the battles of life and sings a song of victory over you. With Christ as your strength, you can not only make it through the battle, but you can come out as a joyful victor.

What does your song of victory sound like?

REFLECTIONS OF THE WEEK

DAY 260

Your Refuge

Trust in him at all times, you people; pour out your hearts to him,
for God is our refuge.

PSALM 62:8 NIV

Pour out your heart to God and rest in his embrace because he is your refuge. No matter what is going on around you, he offers you peace. He can handle all of your emotions, doubts, and insecurities. At all times, he is a safe place.

How has God been your refuge?

DAY 261

Stronghold

The LORD is good,
A stronghold in the day of trouble.

NAHUM 1:7 NKJV

When trouble comes, God is on your side. He is your stronghold. He is your safe place. Whether your trouble is external or internal, God is your strength. He is faithful to protect you from enemies and from your own weaknesses.

How has God been your stronghold in recent times??

DAY 262

Most Beautiful of All

Here's the one thing I crave from God, the one thing I seek above all else:
I want the privilege of living with him every moment in his house.

PSALM 27:4 TPT

God's home is more lovely than you can imagine. It is better than the most beautiful place creation has to offer. When life is overwhelming, remember that better things are coming. One day, you will dwell with God, forever.

What is the most beautiful to you about God?

DAY 263

He Delights in You

"He will take great delight in you;
in his love he will no longer rebuke you."

ZEPHANIAH 3:17 NIV

You are likely no stranger to making mistakes. The list of ways in which you believe you fall short is endless. How glorious that God does not see all of your wrongs! He longs to have compassion and to extend forgiveness to all of his children.

Do you truly believe that God delights in you? Why or why not?

DAY 264

Safety Guaranteed

You will be guarded by God himself.
You will be safe when you leave your home and safely you will return.

PSALM 121:7 TPT

Where do you look for safety? Do you make sure your bank account has a certain balance? Is your house equipped with cameras? Maybe you have excellent insurance. All of these things can be wise and good, but at the end of the day, God is the one who keeps you safe.

How safe do you feel with God?

DAY 265

Answered Prayers

Now I have an answer for my enemies;
I rejoice because you rescued me.

1 SAMUEL 2:2 NLT

Hannah had waited a long time for a son. In this passage she was rejoicing in all that God had done for her. It is good and right to take notice when prayers are answered. Thank God for rescuing you out of situations and giving you an answer for your enemies.

What answered prayers can you thank God for today?

DAY 266

Embracing Weakness

Humble yourselves in the sight of the Lord,
and He will lift you up.

JAMES 4:10 NKJV

Weakness isn't something to be feared or hidden; weakness submitted to God allows the power of Christ to work in and through you. God's love allows you to embrace your weakness, yield it to him, and transform it into something that glorifies him.

What weakness have you embraced for God's glory?

REFLECTIONS OF THE WEEK

DAY 267

Good Things

He fills my life with good things.
My youth is renewed like the eagle's!

PSALM 103:5 NLT

God has filled your life with good things. Have you taken the time to notice? It's easy to focus on what you are lacking or what you wish you had. Instead, ask him to open your eyes to all that is good around you. If you pay attention, you will see God's hand everywhere.

What good things do you see around you?

DAY 268

The Plan

By faith Abraham… obeyed and went, even though he
did not know where he was going.

HEBREWS 11:8 NIV

God's will for your life is not always going to be crystal clear. In your limited understanding, you won't always see what he is doing. It's not your job to make sense of everything, just trust what he is doing and look to him for each step you take.

Can you surrender the plan to God?

DAY 269

Seek Him

Even there you can look for the LORD your God, and you will find him if you look for him with your whole being.

DEUTERONOMY 4:29 NCV

When you look for God, you will find him. He will not withhold himself from the child who asks. He is not hiding from you. He longs to be close to you. Seek him out today and you will not be disappointed.

How do you seek God?

DAY 270

Worthy of Praise

"You are worthy, O Lord,
To receive glory and honor and power."

REVELATION 4:11 NKJV

Worship is a natural response to the goodness of God. It's an opportunity to acknowledge all that he's done and has promised to do. In response to your worship, he gives you peace, joy, and contentedness.

What are you praising God for right now?

DAY 271

Turn Your Eyes

Your eyes will see the King in His beauty;
They will behold a far-distant land.

ISAIAH 33:17 NASB

On the difficult days when your faith is weak, your tears flow freely, and your heart is discouraged, seek the Lord. Turn your eyes to your King and focus on his beauty. In his presence you will find peace. He is faithful to comfort his children and give them hope.

How can you turn your eyes to Jesus today?

DAY 272

Unhindered

Because of Christ and our faith in him, we can now come
boldly and confidently into God's presence.

EPHESIANS 3:12 NLT

Jesus is the reason that you can approach God unhindered. With sin no longer dividing you from his holy presence, you are free to bare your soul to God as his beloved child. Go to him with confidence. You are welcome in his presence.

What does it look like to you to go unhindered to the Father?

DAY 273

Your Purpose

Only let each person lead the life that the Lord has assigned to him, and to which God has called him. This is my rule in all the churches.

1 Corinthians 7:17 ESV

God has plans for your life and purposes for your talents. He created you in a specific way. If you ask him, he will be faithful to show you. He delights in his children living the way that he intended.

How does your life honor God?

REFLECTIONS OF THE WEEK

DAY 274

In the Wilderness

He found them in a desert, a windy, empty land. He surrounded them and brought them up, guarding them as those he loved very much.

DEUTERONOMY 32:10 NCV

God sees you in the wilderness. You have his attention. He has never turned away from you. Even when you feel lost, he is near and knows exactly what you need. Turn to him and wait with expectation. He will lift you up in his perfect timing.

What wilderness have you been wandering in?

DAY 275

Well Equipped

May our Lord Jesus Christ himself and God our Father… encourage your hearts and strengthen you in every good work and word.

2 THESSALONIANS 2:16-17 CSB

No matter what lies before you today, God is on your side. He is ready and able to give you the strength you need. He will equip you to accomplish every good work that he has for you.

What good work do you need to be equipped for?

DAY 276

Filling the Emptiness

O God, you are my God;
earnestly I seek you; my soul thirsts for you.

Psalm 63:1 ESV

Deep in the heart of every person is an innate need for intimacy with the Creator. Without it, souls are thirsty and empty. God alone can satisfy that thirst. Without him, you will constantly search for fulfillment. His nearness is all you need.

What emptiness can God fill for you today?

DAY 277

You Make Him Happy

It has pleased the Lord
to make you a people for himself.

1 Samuel 12:22 ESV

God is pleased by his people. He is proud of you and is delighted by who you are. You have the adoration of the Creator of the universe. You are the object of his affection. When you truly realize this, you won't search for approval anywhere else.

Do you believe that you make the Lord happy?

DAY 278

Strength in Waiting

They who wait for the LORD
shall renew their strength.

ISAIAH 40:31 ESV

It's not always easy to wait. Sometimes waiting on the Lord means biting your tongue or not getting involved in a situation when you want to. Instead of taking control, submit to God's timing and try to be patient. God promises that those who wait on him will be strengthened.

How can you practice waiting on the Lord?

DAY 279

Grief Matters

You yourself have recorded my wanderings.
Put my tears in your bottle. Are they not in your book?

PSALM 56:8 CSB

Your grief matters to God. He longs to console you. He sees you when you toss and turn; he collects your tears. He isn't absent in your sorrow; rather, the opposite. He is closer than ever.

What grief are you walking through today?

DAY 280

True Rest

"Come to me, all you who are weary and burdened,
and I will give you rest."

MATTHEW 11:28 NIV

No matter the burdens you carry, God wants to give you rest. He doesn't expect you to walk through life weary and weighed down. He longs to help you and to lessen your load. Cast your cares upon him and let him help you.

Are you looking for true rest?

REFLECTIONS OF THE WEEK

DAY 281

Ask Seek Knock

"Ask and it will be given to you; seek and you will find; knock and the door will be opened to you."

MATTHEW 7:7 NIV

Don't let your disappointments cloud the truth of God's Word. He promises that everyone who asks in his name receives. When the answer isn't what you want, do you assume that God hasn't heard you? Instead of losing faith, ask God to give you his perspective.

How are you asking, seeking, and knocking?

DAY 282

The Process

Put on your new nature, and be renewed as you learn to know your Creator and become like him.

COLOSSIANS 3:10 NLT

While salvation is a completed work, there is a continual working out of your faith. When you turned to God for the first time, he began a work in your heart that will continue for all of your days. He will be faithful to keep moving in your life.

What has the sanctification process been like for you?

DAY 283

Humble Heart

"Let any one of you who is without sin
be the first to throw a stone at her."

JOHN 8:7 NIV

It's really easy to have a critical spirit toward those around you. Pointing out the flaws of others can take the focus off your own. Ask God to give you a humble heart instead of picking out all that's wrong with other people.

What does having a humble heart look like to you?

DAY 284

Greater Works

"Most assuredly, I say to you, he who believes in Me, the works that I do
he will do also; and greater works than these he will do."

JOHN 14:12 NKJV

Jesus promised that those who follow him will do even greater works than he did. This is encouraging news! You can trust that the same power available to Jesus is available to you.

What big things are you believing God for?

DAY 285

Perfect Ways

God's way is perfect.
All the LORD's promises prove true.

PSALM 18:30 NLT

God's way is perfect. Do you really believe it? When things don't turn out the way you want, does your faith waiver? When life brings sorrow and suffering, do you doubt God? Ask God to help you trust in his perfection no matter what.

How can you trust in the perfect ways of God?

DAY 286

Truth over Feelings

Put your hope in God, for I will still praise him,
my Savior and my God.

PSALM 43:5 CSB

Sometimes you might need to command your soul to praise the Lord. When feelings of despair are heavy, you must move past how you feel. Let the truth of who God is matter more than your emotions.

What truth are you believing over feelings today?

DAY 287

The Good Shepherd

"I give them eternal life, and they will never perish,
and no one will snatch them out of my hand."

John 10:28 ESV

Jesus is a good shepherd. He cares for you with great skill. He knows exactly what is needed for you to be safe, healthy, and thriving. You can put every aspect of your life into his capable hands. Trust his voice and lean on him for all that you need.

How is Jesus a good shepherd to you?

REFLECTIONS OF THE WEEK

DAY 288

A Clear Way

Despite all these things, overwhelming victory is
ours through Christ, who loved us.

ROMANS 8:37 NLT

Nothing can ever separate you from the love of God. Where there was once an impassable chasm, there is now a clear way. Christ's sacrifice is enough for all of time. His death means that you will forever have access to him.

What clear way do you see ahead?

DAY 289

Perfect Bodies

He will take our weak mortal bodies and change them
into glorious bodies like his own.

PHILIPPIANS 3:21 NLT

You will spend all of your earthly days in a broken body. Though everyone has varying degrees of health, none are living in the perfection that God intended. One day, when Jesus makes all things right, all bodies will be perfect like his.

What are you most looking forward to in your new body?

DAY 290

Asking for Wisdom

Listen carefully to wisdom; set your mind on understanding.
Cry out for wisdom, and beg for understanding.

PROVERBS 2:2-3 NCV

There are countless times in Scripture that God says to be wise. He also says that wisdom is a gift he is always faithful to give. It's not a trick. He says to be wise, and he promises to give you what you need to do it.

What do you need wisdom for today?

DAY 291

Wait Well

You must return to your God.
Maintain love and justice, and always put your hope in God.

HOSEA 12:6 CSB

Wait continually for God. Don't give up on him. Even when things don't turn out the way you want. Even when life is full of suffering. Even when you are overwhelmed with despair. God is faithful beyond anything you can imagine. He will keep all his promises.

What does returning to God look like for you?

DAY 292

Secrets of God

"Can you understand the secrets of God?
Can you search the limits of the Almighty?"

JOB 11:7 NCV

As much as you might like to make sense of the world around you, you cannot always make sense of God. He doesn't follow your rules, and he doesn't fit into your boxes. Learn to be okay with some mystery. Let your faith be strengthened by the fact that you don't know everything.

What secrets of God are you excited to find out about?

DAY 293

True Satisfaction

"I am the bread of life," Jesus told them. "No one who comes to me will ever be hungry, and no one who believes in me will ever be thirsty again."

JOHN 6:35 CSB

Everyone was created with a hunger for God. They were designed with eternity in their hearts. You were meant for more than the world has to offer. The only way to fill that hunger is through the Creator. God is the only remedy that provides true satisfaction.

How does God satisfy your soul?

DAY 294

Confess and Believe

If you confess with your mouth that Jesus is Lord and believe in your heart that God raised him from the dead, you will be saved.

ROMANS 10:9 ESV

The truth of the Gospel is simple and profound. Say out loud that Jesus is Lord and believe in your heart that his death and resurrection saved you from your sin. That's it. There's nothing else you need to add. Rejoice in its simplicity and marvel at its wonder.

When did you confess Jesus as Lord of your life?

REFLECTIONS OF THE WEEK

DAY 295

Good Plans

"For I know the plans I have for you," declares the LORD,
"plans for welfare and not for evil, to give you a future and a hope."

JEREMIAH 29:11 ESV

God knows you, and he knows exactly what you need. He knows your future and he knows how each of your days are intertwined. He sees each complex detail and understands how one moment impacts another. Trust his great wisdom and lean on him for each step you take.

What good plans do you think God has for you?

DAY 296

Child of God

All who are led by the Spirit of God
are children of God.

ROMANS 8:14 NLT

When you submit your life to Jesus Christ, you have the privilege of the Holy Spirit leading you in truth and in action. This Spirit, as Paul describes, is proof that you are adopted into God's family. By faith, you can take hold of your claim as God's precious child.

How are you led by the Spirit of God?

DAY 297

Patient Endurance

Patient endurance is what you need now, so that you will continue to do God's will. Then you will receive all that he has promised.

HEBREWS 10:36 NLT

As you grow in your faith, you will learn how much you need patient endurance. There will be days when you aren't excited about your faith, and you aren't motivated to do the right thing. On those days, don't give up. Ask God to help you endure.

How can you endure patiently today?

DAY 298

Be Wary

Direct my footsteps according to your word;
let no sin rule over me.

PSALM 119:133 NIV

You don't need to live as a slave to sin. If sin is ruling over you, submit it to the Lord. Ask for forgiveness and repent. He will give you exactly what you need to walk in freedom. Use wisdom and be wary of the pitfalls you are prone to.

What are you wary of?

DAY 299

Clear Recipe

The fruit of the Spirit is love, joy, peace, patience,
kindness, goodness, faithfulness, gentleness, self-control.

GALATIANS 5:22-23 ESV

Living by the Spirit might seem ambiguous, but there's a clear recipe for it in Scripture. When you follow the Spirit, you will have clear fruit in your life: love, joy, peace, patience, kindness, goodness, faithfulness, gentleness, and self-control.

How do you live by the Spirit?

DAY 300

Ask for Wisdom

If any of you lacks wisdom, you should ask God, who gives generously to
all without finding fault, and it will be given to you.

JAMES 1:5 NIV

There are likely moments every day that require you to have wisdom. No one can navigate every aspect of life on their own. The good news is that you don't need to. If you need wisdom, ask God. He has promised to give it unsparingly.

When did you last ask for wisdom?

DAY 301

Thirst

"Come, all you who are thirsty, come to the waters;
and you who have no money, come, buy and eat!"

ISAIAH 55:1 NIV

Are you feeling spiritually dry today? Have you been too busy to eat and drink properly to satisfy your soul? Go to God! Tell him about your hunger and let him satisfy your thirst. He has exactly what you need.

What do you need from God today?

REFLECTIONS OF THE WEEK

DAY 302

Valuable

"Don't be afraid; you are more valuable to God
than a whole flock of sparrows."

LUKE 12:6-7 NLT

Not only does your life matter to God, but each tiny detail is important to him. You are his precious, valuable creation. There is nothing in existence that matters more to him than you. He loves you and will be faithful to take care of you for all your days.

What details do you see God caring about in your life?

DAY 303

What God Wants

Do what is right to other people, love being kind to others,
and live humbly, obeying your God.

MICAH 6:8 NCV

Don't make the Christian life too complicated. God's commands are not confusing or difficult. He has not asked too much of you. Walk simply and humbly before your God: obey him and be kind to others.

What does God want from you?

DAY 304

All You Need

By his divine power, God has given us
everything we need for living a godly life.

2 Peter 1:3 NLT

You are not lacking. God has given you everything you need to live a godly life. He isn't demanding. He doesn't give you instructions with no way to follow them. He provides you with everything, so you can honor him.

What do you need to honor God.

DAY 305

A Spacious Place

He brought me out to a spacious place;
he rescued me because he delighted in me.

Psalm 18:19 CSB

Take a moment today and revel in the fact that God delights in you. He knows your weaknesses and flaws, and he rescues you. No one will ever love you as thoroughly and as wonderfully as your Creator. His love is boundless.

Do you feel God's delight for you?

DAY 306

Recorded Wrongs

[Love] does not dishonor others, it is not self-seeking,
it is not easily angered, keeps no record of wrongs.

1 CORINTHIANS 13:5 NIV

Love doesn't keep track of problems. It doesn't count up offenses or store away ammunition for use in future conflict. Love doesn't make lists of faults. Instead, love forgives, thinks the best, and lets go of offense.

Do you keep a record of wrongs?

DAY 307

Give Cheerfully

Each of you should give what you have decided in your heart to give,
not reluctantly or under compulsion, for God loves a cheerful giver.

2 CORINTHIANS 9:7 NIV

If you pay attention, you will always see opportunities to serve others. Sometimes you will be generous with your money. You can also be generous with your time, your words, or your talents. Give cheerfully of whatever God has blessed you with.

How do you practice giving cheerfully?

DAY 308

Faultless

He chose us in him, before the foundation of the world,
to be holy and blameless in love before him.

EPHESIANS 1:4 CSB

There is only one requirement to be close to God. You must only appeal to his Son, Jesus, who steps in on your behalf and petitions for your approval. His death on the cross makes you faultless. You are accepted by God and redeemed by grace.

How does it make you feel to be considered faultless before God?

REFLECTIONS OF THE WEEK

DAY 309

Accept Others

Accept one another, then, just as Christ accepted you,
in order to bring praise to God.

ROMANS 15:7 NIV

Instead of focusing on differences, focus on seeing others the way that God sees them. By accepting others with the same measure of absolute acceptance that Christ extends, you honor God and bring him praise.

How can you show acceptance to others today?

DAY 310

The One

"If he finds it he is happier about that one sheep
than about the ninety-nine that were never lost."

MATTHEW 18:13 NCV

There is no point in your walk with the Lord that you become lumped in with everyone else. God is always delighted by you. He doesn't tire of your devotion. You are as valuable to him now as the day you first turned to him.

Do you feel like God will come looking for you every time you stray?

DAY 311

Greatest Comfort

May your unfailing love be my comfort,
according to your promise to your servant.

PSALM 119:76 NIV

Life is full of pain. Everyone will experience suffering to some degree, at some point. None are immune. When trouble comes, find your greatest comfort in the unfailing love of God. Instead of running to the world's offerings, run to the Lord. Let his love give you hope and endurance.

Where do you go for comfort?

DAY 312

Good Soil

"The one on whom seed was sown on the good soil,
this is the man who hears the word and understands it."

MATTHEW 13:23 NASB

When seeds are put into good soil, they will grow and bear abundant fruit. The same is true in your life. If your heart is soft and receptive to the Lord, the truth of the gospel will grow and bear much fruit. Cultivate humility and teachability in your heart, and you will have good soil.

What kind of soil do you have?

DAY 313

Better than Rubies

Wisdom is better than rubies,
And all the things one may desire cannot be compared with her.

PROVERBS 8:11 NKJV

When God offered Solomon anything he desired, the king responded with a request for wisdom. He knew that wisdom was far more valuable than anything else. As a result, he became the most wise, wealthy, famous, successful king who ever lived.

Why do you think wisdom is compared to rubies?

DAY 314

True Beauty

Do not let your adornment be merely outward—
arranging the hair, wearing gold, or putting on fine apparel.

1 PETER 3:3 NKJV

There's nothing wrong with putting effort into your outward appearance, but who you are inside is far more important than what you look like. Value what is precious to God over how you look.

Where does your true beauty lie?

DAY 315

Strong Oak

They will be called oaks of righteousness,
The planting of the LORD, that He may be glorified.

ISAIAH 61:3 NASB

God can take your darkest days, your heaviest emotions, and give you beauty in exchange. He knows when you are overwhelmed. Give him your burdens. He will not leave you to wither under the weight of the pain in your life. He will strengthen you and lift you up.

What does an oak of righteousness mean to you?

REFLECTIONS OF THE WEEK

REFLECTIONS

REFLECTIONS

DAY 316

Always Greater

Seek the LORD and his strength;
seek his presence continually!

1 CHRONICLES 16:11 ESV

Seek the Lord and his strength. Do not depend on your own ability. No matter how successful you are in any given area of your life, God is still better. There is always room to rely on him and to recognize your need for him.

Where do you see the greatness of God?

DAY 317

The Lord Is Near

The LORD is near to all who call on him,
to all who call on him in truth.

PSALM 145:18 ESV

The Lord is near to all who call on him in truth. He is near to everyone whose heart is genuine before him. There is nothing you need to do but seek him. You don't have to clean yourself up or check off a list of requirements. He is near to you when you want to be near to him.

How near does the Lord feel right now?

DAY 318

Close By

"I live in a high and holy place, but also with the one
who is contrite and lowly in spirit."

Isaiah 57:15 NIV

God is close to those who are humble and lowly in spirit. He is faithful to be near to whoever is aware of their need for him. When you are desperate, weary, tired, and broken, God is near. He will not leave you alone when you call out to him.

Do you recognize your need for Jesus?

DAY 319

True Peace

"I leave you peace; my peace I give you. I do not give it to you as the world does.
So don't let your hearts be troubled or afraid."

John 14:27 NCV

God's peace is not dependent on mood or circumstance. His peace is inward and lasting. It's a lack of fear. It's the absence of anxiety. It's the knowledge that no matter what loudness, what weariness, what complications surround you, you are held.

Where can you find true peace?

DAY 320

His Perspective

The LORD will fulfill his purpose for me;
your steadfast love, O LORD, endures forever.

PSALM 138:8 ESV

When it feels more like you're surviving than thriving, God comforts you with the promise that he will complete the work he began in you. He is very aware of you and very capable of helping you fulfill your purpose. Turn to him and ask for his perspective.

Have you asked for God's perspective lately?

DAY 321

Careful Words

Do not speak evil against one another, brothers. The one who speaks against a brother or judges his brother, speaks evil against the law and judges the law.

JAMES 4:11 ESV

Don't speak out against others. Don't slander or gossip or share frustrations with people who aren't involved; it won't make things better. In fact, it only makes things worse. Submit your relationships with others to the Lord and ask for his perspective.

How are you careful with your words?

DAY 322

Faithful

I will remember the deeds of the LORD;
yes, I will remember your wonders of old.

PSALM 77:11 ESV

When you find yourself doubting God's power to work in your life, remember the wonders he has already performed. Scripture is full of accounts of lives changed by the power of God. Even in your own life, there are countless instances when God has been faithful.

When did God show his faithfulness to you last?

REFLECTIONS OF THE WEEK

DAY 323

Lift Up the Needy

"Because of the moans of the helpless,
I will give them the help they want."

PSALM 12:5 NCV

God's economy is completely opposite to the world's. The currency of the world is money and power; God's is mercy and grace. Society elevates the rich and prominent; God lifts up the needy and nameless.

How can you lift up the needy today?

DAY 324

Fully Devoted

"Where you go I will go, and where you stay I will stay.
Your people will be my people and your God my God."

RUTH 1:16 NIV

Ruth gave up everything she'd ever known to follow Naomi back to Bethlehem. What a radical commitment: to leave everything familiar for the sake of devotion to another! When you are fully devoted to God, his blessing and favor will be evident in your life.

Are you willing to leave everything you love and know to follow God?

DAY 325

Empathy

Rejoice with those who rejoice,
weep with those who weep.

ROMANS 12:15 ESV

Empathy is powerful. When you meet people where they are, you communicate that what they are feeling is important. Ask God for the grace to notice how other people feel and to love them well.

How can you have more empathy for those around you?

DAY 326

Good Influence

Do not conform to the pattern of this world,
but be transformed by the renewing of your mind.

ROMANS 12:2 NIV

As a follower of Jesus, you aren't meant to look like the rest of the world. Instead, you imitate the way that Jesus lived. Pay attention to areas of your life where you've let the world's ideas creep in. Ask God to give you a soft heart and a spirit willing to learn.

How can you be a good influence on others?

DAY 327

A Vital Part

In Christ we, though many, form one body,
and each member belongs to all the others.

ROMANS 12:4-5 NIV

There is not one single part of the body that isn't important. If you are feeling useless or unseen, ask God to reveal to you what part you play. You are valuable, needed, and vital to the health of the Body.

What vital part do you play in the Body of Christ?

DAY 328

He Understands

Trust in the LORD with all your heart,
and do not lean on your own understanding.

PROVERBS 3:5 ESV

God's understanding is infinite! He sees each person, situation, generation, and conflict with complete perfection. He knows exactly how everything works together for his glory. Instead of focusing on your own ability to understand, trust that he knows best.

Do you trust God to understand?

DAY 329

Strong in Weakness

No one can measure the depths of his understanding.
He gives power to the weak and strength to the powerless.

ISAIAH 40:29 NLT

When you are lacking, God's power is revealed. When you are tired, he is strong. When you are overwhelmed, he is steady. When you are confused, he is full of understanding. Trust in his ways over your own. He is faithful to lead you the right way.

How is God strong in your weakness?

REFLECTIONS OF THE WEEK

DAY 330

Requirements for Worship

"Offer God a sacrifice of thanksgiving
And pay your vows to the Most High."

Psalm 50:14 nasb

The Israelites in the Old Testament had a complicated list of rituals and sacrifices to follow. When Jesus came, the old requirements were no longer needed. You don't need to follow specific practices to worship God. You can simply let your heart overflow in praise.

How can you praise God today?

DAY 331

Redeemed and Free

He has sent me to proclaim
liberty to the captives.

Isaiah 61:2 esv

Jesus is the great rescuer! He came to set you free. He came humbly as a baby and carried your burdens for you. He freed you from the power of sin and death forever. Praise him today for being such a wonderful redeemer!

What does it feel like to be redeemed and free?

DAY 332

Refreshing

"The water I will give him will become a well of water
springing up in him for eternal life."

John 4:14 CSB

The truth of the gospel is refreshing and invigorating. When you fill your heart with this truth, you will never thirst again. If you find yourself feeling dissatisfied, empty, or constantly searching for more, ask God to renew his spirit within you.

Do you need to be refreshed again?

DAY 333

He Gives Rest

"Everyone, come to me! Are you weary, carrying a heavy burden?
Then come to me. I will refresh your life, for I am your oasis."

Matthew 11:28 TPT

Admit your weakness and ask God for his strength. He is faithful to give rest to the weary. It's not his desire for you to be trudging through life overwhelmed. Let him carry your burdens. Let him renew your spirit.

What do you need from God today?

DAY 334

All You Need

Bless the LORD, O my soul,
and forget not all his benefits.

PSALM 103:2 ESV

God knows exactly what you need at any given moment. Instead of searching for all the world has to offer, go to him. He is the source of all goodness. He has redeemed you, crowned you, and renewed you.

How can you bless the Lord today?

DAY 335

Faithful Affection

"Arise, my love, my beautiful one,
and come away."

SONG OF SOLOMON 2:10 ESV

God's affection for his children is unending. His attention is always on his creation. He loves you and will be faithful to pursue you all of your days. Turn to him and receive the love that he so abundantly gives.

Do you sense the faithful affection of Jesus?

DAY 336

Weight of Worry

Anxiety in a man's heart weighs him down,
but a good word makes him glad.

PROVERBS 12:25 ESV

When you let yourself be carried away by anxiety, you'll quickly lose sight of what's true. God is gracious, compassionate, and fully capable of handling all of your worries. Cast your cares on him and let your heart be light.

What weight do you need to give to God today?

REFLECTIONS OF THE WEEK

DAY 337

Childlike Faith

"I thank you, Father… that you have hidden these things from the wise and understanding and revealed them to little children."

MATTHEW 11:25 ESV

A child's faith in God knows no doubt. They believe that he is who he says he is, and he will do what he says he will do. Their faith is simple and sincere. You can have that kind of faith too.

How could your faith be more childlike?

DAY 338

Help in Battle

When you are tempted, he will also provide a way out so that you can endure it.

1 CORINTHIANS 10:13 NIV

Maybe you wrestle with anger or greed. Perhaps your struggle is with pride or vanity. Whatever your battle, you don't fight alone. God is faithful to help when you need it. Lean on him and he will give you endurance.

What battle are you fighting today?

DAY 339

Equal under Grace

As those who have been chosen of God, holy and beloved, put on a heart of compassion… bearing with one another, and forgiving each other.

COLOSSIANS 3:12-13 NASB

You and your enemies have an equal need for the grace and forgiveness that God offers. Be kind to those around you. You are not better than your brother. Bear each other's burdens with love and grace.

How can you show kindness to those around you?

DAY 340

Faithful Deliverer

The LORD is my rock and my fortress and my deliverer,
My God, my rock, in whom I take refuge.

PSALM 18:2 NASB

No matter what life brings your way, Jesus is your ultimate support. He is your rock. He is your pillar of strength when you feel unsteady and uncertain. When you cry out for help, he is your comfort. He will always be faithful to deliver you and keep you safe.

What do you need to be delivered from?

DAY 341

Live with Integrity

Let integrity and uprightness preserve me,
For I wait for You.

Psalm 25:21 NKJV

In Christ, you are made whole and complete, free from any blemish and stain. You can live a life of integrity because he did. The power available to him is available to you. When you follow his ways, you will live like he did.

How can you live with integrity?

DAY 342

Finished Work

In Him we have redemption through His blood, the forgiveness of our trespasses, according to the riches of His grace.

Ephesians 1:7-8 NASB

Through the blood of Jesus Christ, you are forgiven, set free, and released of the burden of your mistakes. You are given a clean slate. This great gift is free and without requirement. There is nothing you need to do in order to be made clean. Jesus has done the work already.

How can you embrace God's work in your life today?

DAY 343

Reflect Jesus

"May they experience such perfect unity that the world will know that you sent me and that you love them as much as you love me."

JOHN 17:23 NLT

When the church operates in unity, the world will see Jesus. When you love well and keep your eyes fixed on Jesus, those around you will see the love of God. You have the distinct honor of reflecting who God is.

How do you reflect the love of Jesus?

REFLECTIONS OF THE WEEK

DAY 344

Unrealistic Expectations

I am certain that God, who began the good work within you,
will continue his work until it is finally finished.

PHILIPPIANS 1:6 NLT

Be encouraged that sanctification is a process. You aren't expected to be perfect. God is faithfully working in you, transforming you into his likeness. You are not done, and you have not fully arrived. Let this truth set you free from the burden of your own unrealistic expectations.

What expectations do you have for yourself?

DAY 345

No Shame

Those who look to him are radiant,
and their faces shall never be ashamed.

PSALM 34:5 ESV

Those who look at the Lord are not ashamed because they see him and themselves rightly. A child is not ashamed of their fear. Instead of being embarrassed, confidently give your fear to the only one who can handle it.

Are you ashamed in any area?

DAY 346

Good Friends

Perfume and incense bring joy to the heart,
and the pleasantness of a friend springs from their heartfelt advice.

Proverbs 27:9 niv

Sharing life with a faithful friend is one of the true joys that God has given. It is delightful to be able to walk alongside someone in friendship. If you have this joy in your life, thank the Lord. If you don't, ask him for it!

Who can you thank God for today?

DAY 347

Seek His Face

My heart says this about you: "Seek his face."
Lord, I will seek your face.

Psalm 27:8 csb

Seek God's face, and you will find it. Search for him, and you won't be left wanting. He is not hiding from you. He wants to be close to you. The effort you put forth will be matched and exceeded.

How are you seeking after God?

DAY 348

Fully Known

"I chose you before I formed you in the womb;
I set you apart before you were born."

Jeremiah 1:5 CSB

God knows you full well. He is aware of each part of you. He knows all of your strengths and all of your weaknesses. He is your true home. He has called you to do something specific to you. Embrace being fully known today!

How does God feel like your true home?

DAY 349

Inner Beauty

You should clothe yourselves instead with the beauty that comes from within,
the unfading beauty of a gentle and quiet spirit, which is so precious to God.

1 Peter 3:4 NLT

God's Word says that true beauty is found in a gentle and quiet spirit. The world is obsessed with the need to be younger, firmer, stronger, and more stylish. Instead of feeling inadequate, remember that true beauty has nothing to do with what you look like.

How do you define beauty?

DAY 350

Brokenness

The LORD is close to the brokenhearted;
he rescues those whose spirits are crushed.

PSALM 34:18 NLT

Broken things are usually considered worthless and are thrown away. God does not see brokenness the way you do. It isn't impossible or disheartening. He is faithful to fix what is broken and has unlimited resources to do it.

Where do you need fixing?

REFLECTIONS OF THE WEEK

DAY 351

Choosing Contentment

Yet true godliness with contentment
is itself great wealth.

1 Timothy 6:6 NLT

It's easy to fall into the trap of materialism. The world is full of shiny, attractive things. It's important to see the lure of the world for what it is—fleeting and unimportant. Focus on what really matters. Spend your life considering what is eternal.

How do you choose contentment?

DAY 352

Like Him

They took note that these men
had been with Jesus.

Acts 4:13 NIV

Peter and John spent time with Jesus and then went on to do extraordinary things. Those who saw them were very aware of where their power had come from. The same is true now. The more time you spend with Jesus, the more you will be like him.

How could you be more like Jesus?

DAY 353

No Longer a Slave

It is for freedom that Christ
has set us free.

GALATIANS 5:1 NIV

Jesus has set you free! You don't need to live in bondage to sin and death. Remember that his work on the cross is complete and ever sufficient. There is nothing more you need to do to be free. You don't need more discipline or better habits. You are as free now as you will ever be.

Do you feel like you have been set free?

DAY 354

All Things

I can do all things through Him
who strengthens me.

PHILIPPIANS 4:13 NASB

When Paul talks about being able to do all things through Christ, he is referring to being content no matter what is going on around him. You too have this power. No matter what is going on in your life, you have the strength, through Jesus, to be steady and unshaken.

What do you need God's strength for today?

DAY 355

Not Far

"I will live with them and walk among them,
and I will be their God, and they will be my people."

2 Corinthians 6:16 niv

You do not serve a far-off God. He did not create you and then step away to be uninvolved. God loves to be near his children. He wants to be close to you. He cares about your life, and he wants to be a part of each moment of your day.

How near does God feel to you today?

DAY 356

Hearts Aligned

Put your hope in God, for I will yet praise him,
my Savior and my God.

Psalm 42:5 niv

When you place your hope in Christ, every longing will be fulfilled. God knows what you really need. When you align your heart with his, you will not be disappointed. Turn toward him and ask him for his perspective on your life.

How can you align your heart with God's?

DAY 357

Steady and Unwavering

He will respond to us as surely as the arrival of dawn
or the coming of rains in early spring.

Hosea 6:3 NLT

You do not doubt that the sun will rise. You do not doubt that spring will come after winter, or that rain will come, or wind will blow. In the same way, let your faith in the Lord be just as steady and unwavering.

Is your faith steady?

REFLECTIONS OF THE WEEK

DAY 358

Awaited Messiah

"Give glory to God in heaven, and on earth let there be peace among the people who please God."

LUKE 2:14 NCV

Christ came to redeem everyone from the power of sin and death. He destroyed sin and silenced the enemy, permanently, on the cross. The awaited Messiah came and brought peace. He came in humility and made a way for you to be with God.

How do you celebrate the awaited Messiah?

DAY 359

The Best Gift

"She will give birth to a son, and you are to give him the name Jesus, because he will save his people from their sins."

MATTHEW 1:21 NIV

As prophesied and foretold, the promised Messiah finally came and saved mankind from despair. You were once separate from God, but now you have the hope of closeness. He truly is the best gift of all.

How do you thank God for his wonderful gift?

DAY 360

Greatest Gift

"God did not send his Son into the world to condemn the world,
but to save the world through him."

JOHN 3:17 NIV

God could easily stand and point out all your flaws, and he would be justified in doing so. The discrepancy between his perfection and your flaws is great and obvious. But he looks at you with mercy. He didn't send his Son to condemn you but to save you.

How does God's mercy stand out to you today?

DAY 361

Hope in Jesus

"The Root of Jesse will spring up, one who will arise to rule over the nations;
in him the Gentiles will hope."

ROMANS 15:12 NIV

Take a moment today to quiet your heart. A child was born so that you would be free. Fully God and fully man, Jesus brought hope to people who were overwhelmed and full of despair. He is your greatest gift, your eternal salvation.

Where does your hope lie today?

DAY 362

Power to Transform

We are made right with God by placing our faith in Jesus Christ.
And this is true for everyone who believes, no matter who we are.

ROMANS 3:22 NLT

God has the power to transform anything. You may think that a person or situation is completely beyond redemption, but God can reclaim even the most impossible of hearts and circumstances. You may have lost faith in believing for something, but God never does.

What transformation power do you want to see today?

DAY 363

Taking Account

"Where your treasure is,
there your heart will be also."

LUKE 12:34 NIV

If you want to know what's most important in your life, look at where you spend your time and your money. Those two things will quickly reveal what your true priorities are. If they don't align with what you want, or what God wants, ask for his help to shift them.

Where do your priorities lie?

DAY 364

Abundant Life

"I came that they may have life,
and have it abundantly."

JOHN 10:10 NASB

Jesus came to give abundant life. He didn't come to earth as a humble baby just to grow up and tell you about all of your shortcomings. He came to seek and save the lost. He came to bring hope and new life.

What does abundant life look like to you?

DAY 365

God Sees

Remember that the Lord will reward each one of us
for the good we do.

EPHESIANS 6:8 NLT

Don't fall into the trap of thinking that your ministry must be grand. God sees every little act of goodness and love. The water given to the thirsty and a small encouraging word counts just as much as a well delivered sermon or a revival call. God sees all that you do.

What can you do to show the love of God to others?

REFLECTIONS